MANAGING YOUR EMOJIS

100 DEVOTIONS FOR NAVIGATING YOUR FEELINGS

MICHELLE NIETERT, LPC-S, AND LYNN COWELL

ZONDER**kidz**

ZONDERKIDZ

Managing Your Emojis
Copyright © 2023 by Michelle Nietert and Lynn Cowell

Requests for information should be addressed to:
Zonderkidz, *3900 Sparks Dr. SE, Grand Rapids, Michigan 49546*

ISBN 978-0-310-14423-6 (hardcover)
ISBN 978-0-310-14425-0 (audio)
ISBN 978-0-310-14424-3 (ebook)

Library of Congress Cataloging-in-Publication Data

Cover Design: Micah Kandros
Interior Design: Denise Froehlich

Printed in India

23 24 25 26 27   REP   10 9 8 7 6 5 4 3 2 1

From Michelle

To my son Nolan, I love the way you manage your emojis. I'm so grateful for your help with this book, stopping often to give me your kid perspective. Thank you for inspiring me with your kind words of affirmation that delight my mama's soul. Not sure I'm always the "best mom ever" but I have no doubt God knew I was the best mom for you. God has great plans for your quick mind and sensitive heart. (Jeremiah 29:11) Love you to the moon and back and back and back, Mom

• • • •

From Lynn

To Shelby, Mariah, and Madison, the Cowell women who are investing in people's lives each day through counseling and social work. Thank you for all you do for people and all you have taught me about better understanding our emotions. Love, Mom

CONTENTS

Introduction vi

How to Use *Managing Your Emojis* 1

Sad—Embracing Hope
Meditation Matters 3
Devotions 1–25 4–53

Scared—Embracing Brave
Meditation Matters 55
Devotions 1–25 56–105

Mad—Embracing Calm
Meditation Matters 107
Devotions 1–25 108–157

Happy—Embracing Joy
Meditation Matters 159
Devotions 1–25 160–209

How to Begin a Relationship with Jesus 210

About the Authors 212

INTRODUCTION

Hi! I'm Michelle and I've been counseling kids and their families for over 25 years. I am so excited someone gave you this book because I know how hard it is to manage your emotions. But the emotions you feel are energy in motion and with God's help, they can be managed.

You can sense this energy moving through your mind, heart, and body. We wrote *Managing Your Emojis* to teach you about your emotions, help you connect with God, and involve Him in the process of managing feelings, even the ones that catch you by surprise.

What we think often affects what we feel and how we feel often affects what we do. Our mind, heart, and body are all connected. As a Christian counselor, I know that God's Word has lots of solutions for managing our emotions. Lynn and I can't wait to share the solutions we've discovered in the Bible.

We also want to help you discover ways to begin training your brain so it can help you manage your emotions. I am betting you have trained it to learn math facts by practicing almost daily. Just like training your brain to learn math, you can train it to learn God's Word. Learning God's Word and training your brain to focus on His promises can help you over time to replace your feelings of sadness, fear, and anger with hopefulness, bravery, and calmness.

Know we are praying for you as face your feelings and learn to Manage Your Emojis.

Michelle

· · · ·

Hi, Friend! I'm Lynn! I'm so excited you're joining Michelle and me on this journey to discover how we can partner with God to manage our emotions.

I have lots of people in my family who work with others to help them live their lives better. They've been teaching me about my emotions which is making my life better too. I hope that as Michelle and I share truths from God's Word plus examples from our own experiences, you'll find just what you need to embrace and manage the emotions God has given you too.

His,

Lynn

HOW TO USE
MANAGING
YOUR EMOJIS

STEP 1: Read

Each day, you'll find a devotion that begins with a Bible verse. Read the devotion—but take your time! Let God speak to you through the words on each page. If something interesting stands out, grab a pen or highlighter and mark it so you will remember it later!

STEP 2: Embracing

When you've finished reading, you'll see a section called "Embracing." This part will help you apply what you read to your own life. It might ask you a question, give you something to write about or draw, or offer a thought for the day. If you can't answer the question right away, that's OK! Come back to it when you're ready. This is to help you use what we're discussing in the devotion in your life. It's God's Word coming alive in you and through you.

STEP 3: Giving Your Emotion to God

After you've completed "Embracing," the last section is called "Giving Your Emotion to God." This is when you can talk to

God, give your emotions to Him, and turn to Him with the knowledge that He loves you in the midst of these emotions.

This section includes a prayer. If you feel led to pray more than what's written on the page, go for it! This section is to help you grow more confident in talking with God.

At the beginning of each section (on pages 3, 55, 107, 159) you'll see a page called "Meditation Matters." Meditation is training your mind to focus on something with your full attention. When you meditate or think about a Scripture, it's a really cool way to connect with God! You might even wish to focus on the meaning of certain words so you can grow your understanding of the verse. You can refer back to these pages each time you finish a devotion. When you read and meditate on Scripture over and over again, it will help you memorize it or hide it in your heart so you can use it in your life.

SAD—EMBRACING HOPE

Meditation Matters

"The Lᴏʀᴅ is close to the brokenhearted and saves those who are crushed in spirit.

Pꜱᴀʟᴍ 34:18

"For the Lᴏʀᴅ hears the needy."

Pꜱᴀʟᴍ 69:33

". . . Never will I leave you; never will I forsake you."

Hᴇʙʀᴇᴡꜱ 13:5ʙ

God is our refuge and strength, always ready to help in times of trouble.

Pꜱᴀʟᴍ 46:1 (NLT)

1

NOT INVITED

MICHELLE

"The LORD is close to the brokenhearted and saves those who are crushed in spirit."

PSALM 34:18

I will never forget the first time I found out one of my friends was having a sleepover and I wasn't invited. I wondered if I'd done something wrong. I remember thinking, *Wasn't I nice enough, fun enough, or good enough to be included?* It was one of the first times I remember my heart feeling like it was broken.

When our emotions are strong, we feel them in our bodies. Sometimes they flow through tears. Other times our chest gets so tight it hurts. I remember coming home from school after hearing those girls talk about all the fun they planned to have, throwing myself on the bed, and having a good cry. It was a hard day.

My cat came alongside me on the bed and I felt her love and warmth. I probably talked with her and told her how unfair life was and how mad and hurt I felt.

My cat provided comfort but I wish I'd realized then that God was also there to provide comfort. Now I have a dog, but I don't usually talk to him about my heartaches. I turn to my

God who loves me so much. He draws close when I experience rejection from others and feel deeply sad.

Embracing Hope

Think back to a time when your heart hurt. Where were you? Who was there? What did you think and feel? Now take a moment to bring God into that picture or scene. What would He say to you? How would He comfort you? In the space below draw what you see or write any words of comfort God might say to you.

....

....

....

....

Giving Your Sad to God

God, when my heart hurts, help me remember I can talk to you and trust you are listening. Amen.

2

YOU ARE MARVELOUS

LYNN

> *"You are the one who put me together inside my mother's body, and I praise you because of the wonderful way you created me. Everything you do is marvelous! Of this I have no doubt."*
>
> **Psalm 139:13-14 (CEV)**

When I'm writing a book for kids your age, I pull out my old journals and read what I wrote when I *was* your age. Sometimes what I find there makes me feel sad.

For instance, in one journal entry, right across the top, two things I did that day were written in bold. The reason this makes me sad is that I know myself. I wasn't just writing down a couple of facts about my day—I wrote the things that determined how I felt about myself.

Some days I still struggle, focusing on what I do and how I look, thinking these things are more important than they are. But I have grown to know this for sure: I am more than what I do and how I look.

King David from the Old Testament was also a writer and wrote in Psalm 139:13-14, "You are the one who put me together inside my mother's body, and I praise you because of the wonderful way you created me. Everything you do is marvelous! Of this I have no doubt."

When David looked in a mirror, he saw good! He saw himself as created in the image of God, his reflection a reflection of God. (Genesis 1:27) If you find yourself sad because you judge yourself based on what you do or what you see, you're not alone. I think we all do sometimes. But take it from me, or better yet, take it from David. You may not see who you are or what you do as amazing, but you are. You are marvelously made, believe it!

Embracing Hope

Read this truth out loud: I am marvelously made! (It's a tongue twister!) Say it again. Then write it on the lines below several times, helping you to own this important truth.

....

....

....

....

Giving Your Sad to God

Father, I can read these words, but only You can help me believe they are true. Help me. In Jesus's name, Amen.

3

WHAT IS YOUR HOPE IN?

MICHELLE

> *"Why, my soul, are you downcast? Why so disturbed within me? Put your hope in God, for I will yet praise him, my Savior and my God."*
>
> PSALM 43:5

"I hope I make the team" is a phrase I often heard as a middle school counselor. Whether for an athletic team, a certain chair in band, a particular choir, or getting cast in a play, we all struggle, want, and hope to succeed. Sometimes we get exactly what we want, but as we get older and competition gets more intense, there are moments when we'll be disappointed.

Sometimes if we try and still don't get what we want, we can begin to feel discouraged. Over time, we become downcast and give up trying because we think, "What's the point?" I meet many kids who have given up. They no longer try to do a good job or participate in activities because they feel they just can't win. Some have lost friendships because those active in after-school activities seem too busy for them. They feel like no one cares, so they sit in their rooms alone.

But you are never alone. God is with you. He is there and He has great plans for your life. Great plans don't mean you will always get what you want but with every closed door, it's like you're waiting in a hallway with God. He will open another door. Sometimes our waiting isn't passive. It's actively knocking on new doors because God wants us to join Him in the process of new beginnings.

Embracing Hope

Lots of kids want everything to be perfect, but in reality this world is broken. Draw a roadmap of your life so far, mapping out hard times and how you got through them. All of our roads will look different but the good news is our journeys are far from finished. Imagine the road ahead. Envision yourself experiencing disappointment and doing these three things:

- ☺ Turning to God with your feelings.
- ☺ Seeking wisdom from others.
- ☺ Deciding if you want to keep moving down the same road or maybe trying something new.

Giving Your Sad to God

God, It's hard for me not to get the things I want. It makes my heart hurt. Sometimes I even feel like I should give up. But I know you have great plans for my life (Jeremiah 29:11). Give me courage to try again to learn the discipline of working hard at being better or the wisdom to know it's time to try something new. Amen.

LIFT MY HEAD

LYNN

> *"But you, LORD, are a shield around me, my glory, the One who lifts my head high. I call out to the LORD, and he answers me from his holy mountain."*
>
> **PSALM 3:3-4**

Have you ever been going about, having a perfectly fine day when *wham . . .* change sneaks up, bringing sadness with it?

When my parents decided we would begin attending a different church, I couldn't believe it! I loved my church. I had grown up and made good friends there. Now I was expected to just leave?

Sundays were no longer the same. Now, not only were my friends not there, but the service was different as well.

I know David understood sadness because of what he wrote in Psalm 3. He had enemies and felt like no one was rooting for him. Then he wrote: "But you, LORD, are a shield around me, my glory, the One who lifts my head high. I call out to the LORD, and he answers me from his holy mountain." (Psalm 3: 3-4) David knows things can begin to turn around in his heart when he calls out to the Lord.

Sometimes decisions are made for us that we can't change or turn around. And while those who make the decisions may seem to not hear or understand us, we can call out to the Lord, asking Him to help. We can ask God to relieve the sadness that comes from life circumstances that are out of our control and help us feel hope again.

Embracing Hope

Sometimes what can help us feel better is a good scream. (I'm not talking about screaming at someone, but blowing off some steam.) Head outside, in a place where you will bother no one, and let out a yell as loud as you can! On the lines below, describe how it felt to scream as loud as you could. How did your body feel? How did you feel after letting off some steam with a scream?

....

....

....

....

Giving Your Sad to God

Father, sometimes I don't like change. Please come
and fill my heart with joy again even when life
seems out of control. In Jesus's name, Amen.

5

ALWAYS LOVED

MICHELLE

"Though my father and mother forsake me, the Lᴏʀᴅ will receive me."

Psᴀʟм **27:10**

"I thought she would always be there for me," I heard as he sat in my office doodling on a piece of paper. Jake was eight years old but since his parents divorced when he was two, he could count the number of times he had seen his mom on one hand.

"What's wrong with me? I try to be a good boy." My heart breaks for kids like Jake. Sometimes because of their past or life choices, parents can't love their kids the way they wish they could. Even though a child has done nothing wrong, they often feel unloved. This can lead to some kids feeling sad and wanting to hide because they think others will see their badness too. For others, they begin working hard to make people like them, even if it means not being themselves.

Most students I've met at one time or another have thought one of their parents was so mad at them he or she no longer loved them. Parents make mistakes. I can be calm in the counseling office when a family is about to explode. But when I am in my role as a parent and am tired, in pain, or overwhelmed, my emotions can well up inside me, exploding on my own children.

One time, when I corrected my daughter for something small, she looked so hurt I asked her, "What did you hear me say?" She replied that she was the worst kid ever. I then had her sit on my lap, and I told her maybe my face looked mad or my voice was loud, but I have never, ever thought anything like that.

Whether our parents try hard to show us love or they don't know how because of their own struggles, we have a heavenly parent who always loves us no matter what. No matter how you feel about yourself or what you've thought or done, He will always receive you. And He will never be too busy. Jesus showed us this when He was on earth, when He said, "Let the little children come to me . . ." (Matthew 19:14).

Embracing Hope

The next time you feel one of your parents no longer loves you, I want to encourage you to talk with them about your feelings when they are smiling and calm. Even if you have a parent whom you feel will never love you like you want to be loved, remember that God loves you and He is always going to be with you.

Giving Your Sad to God

God, thanks for always being the One I can turn to when I'm feeling unloved. Help me experience your love in the thoughts I think and the feelings I feel about myself, even when I'm having a bad day. Amen.

DISAPPOINTED AGAIN

LYNN

> "The Lord is a refuge for the oppressed, a stronghold in times of trouble."
>
> PSALM 9:9

Do you have chores at your house?

Growing up, when my mom gave me a job to do, sometimes I wouldn't get it done. I didn't mean to not obey and not do what she had asked. On the other hand, I didn't intentionally follow through. When that happened, I disappointed her. Sometimes I also got in trouble for not obeying.

How do you feel when you disappoint someone? When I do, my heart feels heavy. I want to fix it and make it right again, but sometimes that isn't possible. The pain I feel in disappointing someone is sometimes worse than any punishment I might be given.

When we have disappointed someone and feel sad, we can't go back and change the past, no matter how we might feel. Think of it like a tube of toothpaste. Once you squeeze out that toothpaste, it's impossible to get it back in. (Try it if you want to! I did and it just doesn't work!) We can, however, purpose in our hearts to do the right thing next time. This decision may not take away our sadness, but it can give us hope for the future.

God tells us we can turn to Him when we are in trouble or oppressed. Oppressed is a big word meaning we feel heavy with thoughts or feelings, like disappointing someone. We can turn to Him when we need a safe place to talk about our sadness. He is that safe place, even when we find ourselves in trouble.

Embracing Hope

Mark this devotion by turning the page corner down or making a colored mark in the corner. When you disappoint someone (and you will because you are human), come back to this page and read Psalm 9:9 out loud.

Giving Your Sad to God

God, thank you for being my safe place when I feel sad. Even though I can't be perfect at this, help me to obey and follow through as often as I can. When I fail, help me find comfort in You. In Jesus's name, Amen.

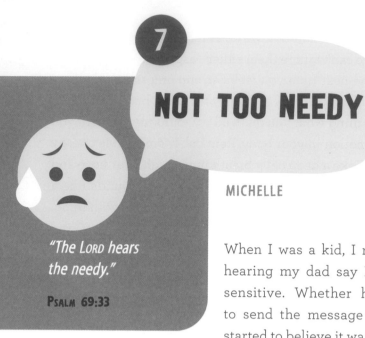

NOT TOO NEEDY

MICHELLE

"The Lord hears the needy."

Psalm 69:33

When I was a kid, I remember hearing my dad say I was too sensitive. Whether he meant to send the message or not, I started to believe it wasn't OK to have lots of feelings. Fortunately, I was surrounded by friends and Sunday school teachers who affirmed my need to express my emotions often. In high school, my pastor validated my ability to know what I'm feeling, express my emotions, and sense other people's emotions. He taught me that these traits described a spiritual gift called "mercy."

Just like my friends and spiritual mentors, God cares about our needs even if others seem too busy or we think our needs aren't important. We can turn to Him when we are sad and pour our hearts out to Him. We can tell Him when someone hurts our feelings. Scripture promises He will hear us! God created each one of us differently. Some of us don't really care what others say or think about us. Others of us are naturally wired to feel more deeply and are more sensitive to sounds, images, and emotions that surround us.

Yes, it's important that we don't let our emotions run our lives, but we can't ignore them either—especially when they're intense. The next time you feel a strong emotion, instead of trying to hide it, let it flow through your mind, body, and heart. Start by naming what you feel and try to discover where you feel that emotion in your body. Remember emotion is energy in motion. Take a deep belly breath in through your nose and out through your mouth, making a noise that sounds like a sigh in your throat. If it still feels stuck, you might try shaking, dancing, wiggling, or stretching out the energy while saying to yourself, "I choose to let my sad, mad, or scared go." Talk to God, asking Him to help you manage your emotion so it's not overwhelming. He's always there; ready to listen. He is your Great Friend and Comforter.

Embracing Hope

The next time you feel the craving for attention, remind yourself God is with you to comfort you and cheer you on. You might try talking to Him out loud or writing out your thoughts and feelings to Him.

Giving Your Sad to God

God, your Word says you are always with us. Sometimes it's hard to believe and I forget. Help me understand that you are with me and for me, especially on hard days. Amen.

SOMEONE, SOMEPLACE, OR SOMETHING

8

LYNN

"In my distress I called to the LORD; I cried to my God for help. From his temple he heard my voice; my cry came before him, into his ears."

PSALM 18:6

When you are feeling sad what is the *first* thing you do?

Some of us run to someone—a friend, a parent, a teacher, or a sibling. But what about those times when *someone* isn't available?

We may run to something that brings us comfort, like a blankie, stuffed animal, or our favorite food or drink.

Other times when we're sad, we go someplace. A place like our bed or a special hideout to feel better.

But what happens when someone, something, or someplace can't be there for us? What then?

David gives us not only some great advice but also a pattern. He says in Psalm 18:6, "In my distress, I called to the LORD; I cried to my God for help. From his temple he heard my voice; my cry came before him, into his ears." David was in a tough place where someone who was supposed to love him became his enemy. The thing that brought him comfort, a musical instrument, couldn't be carried everywhere he went.

And he was on the run from his enemy who was trying to harm him, so he couldn't go to his place of comfort.

One thing David always had with him wherever he went was the Lord. When he was distressed, in great pain, anxiety, or sorrow he knew the Lord heard him. No matter where David was or what was going on, he could cry to the Lord for help.

Embracing Hope

Who is someone you turn to? What is something that brings you comfort? Where is your someplace?

On the lines below write about someone you could turn to if you are upset. In your mind practice what it would be like to talk to them about a problem. You could also imagine turning to something or going somewhere that brings you comfort. Now add God into the picture.

....

....

....

....

Giving Your Sad to God

God, thank you that I can turn to You for help anytime
and anywhere. In Jesus's name, Amen.

LETTING GO OF PAIN

9

MICHELLE

"He will wipe every tear from their eyes. There will be no more death or mourning or crying or pain, for the old order of things has passed away."

Revelation 21:4

Often when I'm counseling kids and grown-ups, as they begin to share their pain, they start to cry. They apologize and grab a tissue to wipe their tears. I let them know my office is a safe place; tears are welcomed during the process of healing and change. God gave us tear ducts and they help us keep our eyes clean. When we feel sad, scared, or mad, our eyes can fill up with extra tears, and like a fountain, they can overflow onto our face. Letting our tears fall helps our body make hormones that make us feel better. These hormones are called endorphins and help us have a sense of calm we wouldn't experience without the tears.

Your life will be filled with both good times and hard ones. It's OK to let out your tears when you've had a bad day. Sometimes, crying and knowing God sees us is what we need to feel better. Other times, crying with someone who cares, listens, and understands brings additional healing. When we hear, "That does sound hard. I can tell you are really disappointed," our sad seems like a natural response and allows us to begin to let the sadness go.

Tomorrow is a new day. If we're grieving a loss in our lives, we may not feel better immediately. But over time, our sadness can shrink little by little as the days pass and happy moments remind us we can have hope that God is for us. If we have chosen to put our faith in Jesus, we will be in heaven with Him someday. Scripture doesn't tell us everything about heaven, but it does tell us we will have no more pain or tears there. I'm looking forward to that. Aren't you?

Embracing Hope

The next time you feel sad and want to cry, remind yourself God gave you crying to help you feel better. Let your tears flow. If you are able, share your sad feelings and let yourself cry with a grownup or friend you trust so they can be God's comfort to you.

Giving Your Sad to God

God, thanks for giving me tear ducts so I can cry and feel better in my body. I'm so glad someday I will be in heaven where my heart won't hurt and I won't need to cry. Amen.

STICKING BY YOU

LYNN

"Friends come and friends go, but a true friend sticks by you like family."

PROVERBS 18:24 (MSG)

I was hoping today would be the day. I heard our school had sent announcements to our parents telling us which class we would be in for third grade. I was hoping I would be in the same class as my best friend.

That day I discovered what I feared.

We weren't in the same class.

Have you noticed when you don't have a certain thing in common it can be harder to keep a friendship going? If you aren't in the same class or on the same team, when you no longer live next door or attend the same church, it can be difficult to be good friends.

That year my best friend and I began to drift apart, which made me feel so sad. Having friends come in and out of our lives can leave us feeling unhappy, especially if some of our friends continue their friendships without us.

Jesus experienced this pain. On the night He was arrested even though He did nothing wrong, almost all of His friends ran away. They didn't want to be in trouble with the people who were mad at Jesus, so they pretended He wasn't their friend.

Proverbs 18:24 tells us, "Friends come and friends go, but a true friend sticks by you like family." (MSG) Jesus is that true friend. He's your brother and will never leave your side, no matter what!

Embracing Hope

Changes in friendships happen to everyone. When you change schools, teams, or get a new cabin at camp, you will be with different people and make new friends. Some friendships are for a short period of time and others might be for your lifetime.

Write a prayer to the Lord in the space below. Thank Jesus for the friends you've had that were good friends, but are no longer with you. Let Him know that you're thankful He is your friend for always.

....

....

....

....

Giving Your Sad to God

Jesus, thank You for sticking close to me. I'm glad there's never a season when You're not my friend. In Jesus's name, Amen.

HOPING IN THE LORD

11

MICHELLE

"But those who hope in the LORD will renew their strength. They will soar on wings like eagles; they will run and not grow weary, they will walk and not be faint."

ISAIAH **40:31**

Hope is important because it prevents our sad feelings from turning into depression. Hope can be tricky though. Many people think hope is looking forward to something in the future. That idea of hope can lead to disappointment because as much as you try, you can't control your future.

When I was younger, I put my hope in getting good grades, winning competitions, how I looked, and who liked me. When I was in middle school, I began to think my life would be better if a certain boy liked me. As I got older, I realized putting my hope in earthly things left me feeling tired and like I was never enough. Can you relate?

The Bible gives us different definitions of hope. It says hope is trusting in God. Because God keeps His promises, we can put our trust in Him.

Putting our hope in anything other than God can make us tired. I meet tweens and teens in the counseling office who are exhausted. They tell me they have no energy no matter how much they sleep. I ask them about their life, their hopes, and dreams to help me understand where they put their hope. I help them begin to put their hope in God and as they do, they report it takes the pressure off them feeling like they have to be perfect.

Embracing Hope

If you don't know many of God's promises, you might want to start learning some. With permission, you might look up Bible verses online or ask someone to share some Scriptures from God's Word they love. This book is filled with them! You might want to choose one from the Meditation Matters in this book. Next, write the verse on the lines below. Then, try to say the verse out loud every day. In our offices, we have kids write their verse on sticky notes they can put in their cubbies, lockers, or notebooks, or put up on their walls or mirrors.

....

....

....

....

Giving Your Sad to God

God, teach me who You are and how I can count on You. I want to put my hope in You instead of in things that I can't control like grades, awards, and how others feel about me. Amen.

12

TAKE HEART

LYNN

> *"I have told you these things, so that in me you may have peace. In this world you will have trouble. But take heart! I have overcome the world."*
>
> JOHN 16:33

"We're going to move," my mom said. Why? My whole world would change if I left my neighborhood friends and I went to a new school.

In John 16, as Jesus was preparing to leave the earth, He spent some time with His disciples, sharing what would take place before He left.

These words may have caused his friends to feel scared and sad. Jesus also shared that even though He wouldn't be with them in person, He would still be with them. He would give them the Holy Spirit that would go with them everywhere. Even though they didn't understand, Jesus was explaining that the Holy Spirit would fill them on a future day the Bible calls Pentecost. Jesus wanted his followers to know that He would be with them when life was hard. He told his friends, "I have told you these things, so that in me you may have peace. In this world you will have trouble. But take heart! I have overcome the world." (John 16:33) Jesus told them to hang in there because, in the end, He would win.

There are things you will wish weren't happening. Maybe

your parents are divorcing, your grandparent is sick, or your pet is going to die. It's hard to hear something bad is coming because we start feeling sad before it happens. Sometimes the sad lasts a long time.

Jesus knows we experience these types of troubles. He was here too. He also promises us He can give us peace even when we're in the middle of sadness. He's always with us and the Holy Spirit is in us.

Embracing Hope

Sometimes when we are sad, our emotions are overwhelming. If we can, it's good to step away from the situation causing us sadness and reset. Try this to help you reset:

- ☺ Lay down and shut your eyes.
- ☺ Picture a favorite place like the beach or your treehouse.
- ☺ Picture yourself feeling what's around you; putting your hand in the sand, or touching the wood of your treehouse.
- ☺ See if you can smell the smells—the ocean breeze or the wood of the treehouse.
- ☺ Listen to the sounds surrounding you like the waves lapping against the sand or the breeze hitting the tree branches.
- ☺ As you "see" this place, what's around you? Palm trees or toys in your treehouse?

Giving Your Sad to God

Jesus, thank you that I am never alone, even
when I feel sad. In Jesus's name, Amen.

13
SOMETIMES SAD MAKES YOU BETTER

MICHELLE

"Godly sorrow brings repentance that leads to salvation and leaves no regret, but worldly sorrow brings death."

2 CORINTHIANS 7:10

As a counselor, every day I talk with kids about sadness. Not all sadness is the same. Sometimes sadness feels like disappointment, such as when you earn a grade lower than you wanted. Sometimes it feels more intense like dejection; when your spirit is low because you feel a friend rejected you. Another type of sadness appears because we live in a broken world and are aware of the misery people experience when they suffer.

We can feel sad due to regret. Regret can come when fear gets in the way and we miss an opportunity to be brave. Sadness can hit us when we realize we made a bad choice, causing us or someone we love to suffer. The Bible talks about this type of sadness as being godly sorrow. If we turn to God with it, we can receive His forgiveness. God can't change the past, but when we receive His forgiveness, we can be freed from guilt that could make us feel stuck.

Embracing Hope

Write down any mistakes you've made recently, causing you to feel guilt or sadness. Thank God for forgiving you of these mistakes that the Bible calls sin. Ask Him to help you make better choices in your future. God is faithful to help us in our struggles when we involve Him in them.

Mistakes I'm Giving to God

....

....

....

....

Giving Your Sad to God

Father, thank You that I can be freed from guilt that comes from the mistakes I've made. Thanks for being the kind of God I don't have to hide from but can turn to even when I've done wrong. You forgive me. Amen.

14
HEALING FOR MY BROKEN HEART

LYNN

"Then know this, you and all the people of Israel: It is by the name of Jesus Christ of Nazareth, whom you crucified but whom God raised from the dead, that this man stands before you healed."

ACTS 4:10

When I was a young woman, my dad died. His death came too early; I wasn't ready to have my father go to heaven—I thought he would be alive until I was much older. My heart was broken. No matter how many times people said words they meant for good, like, "He's in a better place" or "He's with God now," it didn't help. Sometimes their "good" words made me feel worse.

I needed Jesus to heal my broken heart.

In Acts 3:1–9, the disciples of Jesus—Peter and John—are going to the temple to pray. On their way, they see a man with a disability asking for money. Peter doesn't have any money, but he does have hope for the man to be healed by Jesus. And that is exactly what happened!

Later, a group of people ask Peter what happened. They're having a hard time believing this man was healed. Peter tells them. (Acts 4:10)

It would have been kind if Peter and John had said nice words to him and encouraged him to think positively. While their positivity and kindness might have helped the man feel better for a moment, Jesus healing his body changed his life forever!

The same was true for me. I appreciated the kind words and thoughts of others, but the only person who could heal me on the inside was Jesus.

Embracing Hope

Do you have something you need healing for? Jesus healed people when He was on the earth and He is still healing people today. Ask Him to begin the process of healing you and shrinking the hurt in your heart.

Giving Your Sad to God

Jesus, my (fill in the blank) needs healing.
Please heal me. In Jesus's name, Amen.

15

GOD WON'T ABANDON YOU

MICHELLE

"Never will I leave you; never will I forsake you."

HEBREWS 13:5

Recently I was sitting with my family watching a movie where the dad died. The boy missed him and struggled with anger and loneliness. I looked at my son to make sure he was OK because his cousin's dad died when they were young. Watching this sadness in our family hurt my son's heart deeply. The loss made him scared that his father or I might die.

A parent dying is one of the greatest fears most kids experience. As a counselor, I have worked with families where one parent has gone to heaven. Even though the kids believe they will see their dad or mom again, they are heartbroken by grief and loss.

As my son struggled with his fear of one of us dying, we talked about how, no matter what happened, he could turn to God. The Bible promises God will never leave us or forsake us. I explained to my son that God will always be with Him even when I can't. My son can't take me to school with him, and he won't be able to take me to work or college one day, but God can go anywhere he goes. We talked about how he felt safe with me. My son then carried a rock in his pocket as a reminder that God was always with him. The reminder made him feel safe, knowing God was there and could protect him even better than I could. God even sends angels to protect us. (Psalm 91:11)

In the movie, the boy was able to travel back in time and talk to his dad once again. Although we don't currently get to experience time travel, we can practice recognizing God's presence in our lives throughout our day. While His presence won't instantly remove the heartache of someone dying, it can bring us comfort in the middle of our grief knowing we will never be alone.

Embracing Hope

Ask God to open your spiritual eyes so you can recognize His presence throughout your day. You might envision Him with you during every part of your day—as you get dressed, eat meals, walk down halls at school, and beside you at your desk and at recess. Work on recognizing that He is with you as you do your homework or when you're in your room at night and feel alone. Don't worry if it takes time, if you forget, or get distracted. Just start again and over time, it will be easier to sense His presence.

Giving Your Sad to God

God, it's sad when someone we love dies. Thank You that You are eternal and live forever. We will always have You with us because You've promised not to leave or abandon us. Amen.

16

TWO ARE BETTER THAN ONE

LYNN

"Two are better than one, because they have a good return for their labor. If either of them falls down, one can help the other up. But pity anyone who falls and has no one to help them up."

ECCLESIASTES 4:9-10

"Are you ok?" my friend asked me. Quickly I gave the easiest answer, "Yeah, I'm ok."

But the truth was I wasn't. I was really sad. I hadn't shared it with anyone because I was afraid no one would understand. So I carried the sadness alone.

Later that day, my friend asked again. This time I decided to be brave and tell him. He listened, hugged me, and let me cry on his shoulder.

When my friend listened to me, hugged me, and let me get out a good cry, it didn't take away my problem. But it did help me to feel not so alone when I was hurting inside. My friend's compassion helped me keep going even with the sadness in my heart.

Ecclesiastes 4:9-10 tells us, "Two are better than one, because they have a good return for their labor: If either of them falls down, one can help the other up. But pity anyone who falls and has no one to help them up." This is what

I experienced that day. My friend helped me up. Before that could happen, I had to share what was happening with me. If I didn't let him see my sadness and choose to be vulnerable, he would not have known how to comfort me in my pain.

Embracing Hope

Sometimes it's scary sharing about something that hurts us. We can be brave, though, and find someone who is safe to share with. When we do, we open the opportunity for them to help us up. It might help you to write before you share the scary thing. You can do so in the lines below.

....

....

....

....

Giving Your Sad to God

Jesus, thank you that I can always come to you for help.
Please show me another person who is safe for me to
talk to when I am hurting. In Jesus's name, Amen.

WHEN WE FEEL DESPERATE

MICHELLE

"In my desperation I prayed, and the LORD listened; he saved me from all my troubles."

PSALM 34:6 (NLT)

"Mom, I'm desperate." I often hear my kids yell these words when hunting for a shoe, paper, or something they need for school. Sometimes we use emotional words that may seem really intense to others, but in that moment our minds and bodies are experiencing that emotion. I remember one time when I was crying hard, one of my parents said, "Quit being so dramatic." Inside I became angry because I felt misunderstood. Has that ever happened to you?

Sometimes our feelings are intense. When we feel desperate, helpless, or hopeless, our thoughts can begin to race. We may say:

- ☺ I'm just not good enough.
- ☺ I'm never going to be able to do this.
- ☺ I might as well give up.
- ☺ Why even try?

Helpless and hopeless thoughts can create feelings that

leave us stuck. Sometimes we pray to God and we feel like nothing changes.

When I'm overwhelmed, desperate, and feeling like my prayers aren't being answered, I turn to someone I trust and ask them to pray for and with me. I did that today in church. Asking for help takes courage. But I'm so glad I did. I shared how I was feeling with an older woman and she put her hands on my cheeks and spoke words of encouragement over me. By the end of her short prayer, I felt a release and freedom I hadn't found with God by myself.

Embracing Hope

Do you have someone you can ask to pray for and with you? Ask God to show you someone or a few people you can recruit to be on your prayer team—a group of people who pray for you. This person might be one of your parents, an older brother or sister, a friend, or maybe a trusted adult. As a Christian counselor, I often pray with and for my clients. If your list is short, you might ask God to bring some people into your life who will pray for you. A good way to meet them is at church. Another way to grow your list is to ask people how you can pray for them. They might just ask you the same question in return.

Giving Your Sad to God

God, thank You for promising to save me from trouble. I need people in my life You can use to help me when I feel desperate. Help me find them so when trouble comes, I will have not only Your Spirit but others who You can use to pray for and with me. Amen.

18
THANKFUL RATHER THAN BETTER THAN

LYNN

"A peaceful heart leads to a healthy body; jealousy is like cancer in the bones."

PROVERBS 14:30 (NLT)

Seeing the finish line ahead, I gave it everything I had left. Making my way to my coach, he gave me a huge smile. While I didn't win, it was the fastest I had ever run. Grinning from ear to ear, I thought, *I did it!*

After sharing the good news that I had run my fastest time, my coach stepped over to another teammate and shared their time with them. Their time was faster than mine. Suddenly, it didn't matter to me that I had run faster than I ever had. My teammate had run faster than me; now I felt sad.

You know what? I didn't have to feel sad that day. I felt sad because I fell into comparison. I listened to the coach share my teammate's time and I compared it to mine. I decided since their time was faster, mine was no longer good.

Here is some good news: you and I don't have to choose to compare ourselves with someone else. We can avoid it by using the "muscle" of thankfulness. We can make a choice to look at our circumstances and be thankful, rather than looking at others and wishing their experience was ours.

I call this the "muscle" of thankfulness because choosing to be thankful is like working out. When I first started running, I couldn't go very far. Every step felt hard. After practicing for a while, I could run a long way!

The same is true with thankfulness. The more we choose to be thankful instead of choosing to compare, the stronger we will be to avoid comparison's pit.

Embracing Hope

Choose one thing to thank God for right now and write out that thing on the lines below. How does it feel to simply say thank you?

....

....

....

....

Giving Your Sad to God

Jesus, thank you for (fill in the blank.) In Jesus's name, Amen.

19

HELP IN TROUBLED TIMES

MICHELLE

"God is our refuge and strength, always ready to help in times of trouble."

Psalm 46:1 (NLT)

I asked several kids what some times of trouble they have experienced are and below are some of their answers:

Death
Bad grades
A friend no longer wanting to
    be my friend
Hurting my foot
Getting caught for doing
    something bad
Kids being mean at school

Their list of troubles could be sorted into two categories: situations we have some control over and things we can't control at all. For example, if we've done something wrong, avoiding trouble can even lead to more trouble like hiding it or lying to avoid getting caught. When we've done something, we can't go back and change it. We can however be honest in the present and work at changing our future.

The Bible says that trouble in this world is a sure thing

(John 16:33). We can't escape it completely. So when trouble comes your way, what will you do? I know I often get mad or sad first; that's normal. I'm even often tempted to try and ignore the trouble I'm facing. I see lots of kids try and do this; we wish trouble would disappear.

When troubles come, I believe that's when we need God most. He wants to be the one we pour our troubles on. He promises to be a shelter in our storms. That doesn't mean He makes the troubles disappear, but He can help us weather them by calming us on the inside. In Mark 4:35–41, Jesus and His friends are in a bad storm in a boat. Jesus literally calmed the storm so they didn't drown. Just as Jesus calmed the storm when He was on the boat, He can calm the storms in our hearts. He can give you the internal strength to hold on to hope when times are tough. He is ready to help.

Embracing Hope

On a separate sheet of paper write down some troubled times you or your family have faced. Then write out ways God helped you, whether it was through changing something on the outside or giving you strength on the inside to get through them. Next time you're facing overwhelming trouble, look back at this list and be reminded how God is here to help.

Giving Your Sad to God

God, thanks for being ready to help me in times of trouble. I confess that I want you to make the problems better quickly. When that doesn't happen, give me strength to manage my thoughts and feelings, knowing that trouble doesn't last forever. Amen.

WHO IS AT THE DOOR?

LYNN

> *"Be happy with those who are happy, and weep with those who weep."*
>
> ROMANS 12:15 (NLT)

When my doorbell rang, I ran to see who it was and was so excited to see my friend, dropping by to just say "hi." How fun! Yesterday when my doorbell rang, the delivery person had a Christmas present from my parents. It was yummy!

I did have a time though, when the doorbell rang and on the other side were two young people I love and they were crying. Their parents were fighting and they didn't know what to do. I held them in my arms and cried with them.

Opening my front door, I'm never certain what or who will appear. Not knowing what's on the other side of my front door can make me feel a little out of control and when I hear the doorbell ring, I even feel helpless at times.

Our emotions can be like a front door. We have no control over what shows up. There may be a happy arrival one time and a sad one the next. While we can't control what emotions arrive, we can choose how we greet them.

Romans 12:15 tells us: "Be happy with those who are happy, and weep with those who weep" (NLT). That is what I did the day those young people arrived at my door. They needed me to be sad with them; to hold and reassure them that Jesus would not leave them alone. He would help.

When you are feeling sad and you need someone to simply be sad with you, it is ok to let someone know. Sometimes when my children are expressing how they feel, I will ask them, "Do you just need someone to listen right now, or are you wanting advice or help?"

The next time you want to talk with someone about your thoughts and feelings, let them know what you need. If it's someone to simply listen, it's helpful for them to know that expectation as they are listening.

Embracing Hope

Practice saying these words: "I feel sad right now. Can I tell you how I feel? I don't need advice, just someone to listen." It may feel strange at first, but like most things, it will be easier with practice. And the next time someone comes to you with a problem, listen first to understand and then ask them how you can be helpful—whether it's just listening, sharing encouragement or wisdom, or helping them get help from an adult if they need it.

Giving Your Sad to God

Jesus, thank you that when I feel sad, You are always there to listen to how I feel. In Jesus's name, Amen.

21
COMFORTED TO BE A COMFORT

MICHELLE

"All praise to God, the Father of our Lord Jesus Christ. God is our merciful Father and the source of all comfort. He comforts us in all our troubles so that we can comfort others. When they are troubled, we will be able to give them the same comfort God has given us."

2 CORINTHIANS 1:3-4 (NLT)

As I read the Scripture about God comforting us so we can comfort others, it reminds me of a phrase my kids learned at school. "You are blessed to be a blessing." This idea comes from the book of Genesis where a man named Abram is told that everyone on earth will be blessed through him.

I'd like you to think of some ways God has blessed you.

☺ Has He gifted you with certain talents or skills making you good at sports, academics, or fine arts like theater, art, or music?

☺ Has He given you the strength to try again when you mess up?

☺ Has He given you people in your life who listen to you and love you no matter what?

Now let's think of some ways He's comforted you.

- ☺ Does He listen to you when you talk with Him?
- ☺ Do you have a pet who shows God's love and comfort to you?
- ☺ Have you been hugged by someone just when you needed it?

Just as God blesses and comforts you, He wants you to share His blessings and comfort with others.

Embracing Hope

On the lines below, make a list of people you could bless or comfort and how you would plan to do this. Put a star by one of these people and act on your plan this week. You can even come back here and write how it went and how you felt when you shared God's hope.

....

....

....

....

Giving Your Sad to God

God, thanks for comforting me when I'm down. Give me courage to offer comfort to others even if I feel like it might not matter since I'm just a kid. Help me remember everyone matters in Your kingdom. Amen.

HAPPINESS HUNTER

LYNN

"May the righteous be glad and rejoice before God; may they be happy and joyful."

PSALM 68:3

I recently read of a place in Arkansas called Crater of Diamonds State Park. People come from all over, bringing shovels and pails, to look for diamonds. Getting on their hands and knees, they dig through the dirt to find a treasure.

You and I can also be hunters—happiness hunters for when good things occur in our lives.

Sometimes just like digging, we have to spend a little time and effort to uncover happiness. For example, we might be frustrated that it's raining really hard but if we dig a little deeper, we might discover it's fun to splash in a puddle or two. When we are sick with a fever, we might discover that it's comforting to have a parent around who takes good care of us when we don't feel well even if we really wanted to go to school that day. When we really wanted a friend to come over, we might discover having a fantastic time playing with a brother or sister is like uncovering hidden treasure.

In Psalm 68:3 David, the writer of this psalm, says what he's going to do. By saying "may the righteous be glad and rejoice before God" he's making a choice. He's telling us he is a happiness hunter. He's digging for happiness by praising God and giving thanks to Him for being good and loving him so well.

David didn't have a perfect life. He was the king of a huge country and didn't always make the best decisions. Yet he found his happiness in God.

David can be a role model for us in this area. Praising the Lord and giving Him thanks not only stirs up happiness in our hearts, but it gives God the glory He desires and deserves because He is our God!

Embracing Hope

On the lines below take just a moment to be like David and become a happiness hunter. Think about this past week. Write down some ways you uncovered the treasure of God's love and goodness in your life. Make a commitment to be a happiness hunter all the days of your life, even when life is hard and you need to dig and dig before you uncover more treasure.

....

....

....

....

Giving Your Sad to God

Lord, You are great and deserve our praise. Thank you for being good and loving me so well. In Jesus's name, Amen.

POWER IN WEAKNESS

23

MICHELLE

> *"Each time he said, "My grace is all you need. My power works best in weakness." So now I am glad to boast about my weaknesses, so that the power of Christ can work through me."*
>
> 2 CORINTHIANS 12:9

Do you find yourself admiring people who appear strong? Those who have strong personalities and are chosen to lead or seem to get more opportunities?

As I read the verse from 2 Corinthians, it seems confusing to me. Should we try and be weak? I don't think so.

I do think when we are asked to do something hard or something we aren't really good at, we can turn to God and let people know we are depending on Him to help us. When we trust God with our weaknesses, He can give us power. When we succeed, we can also give God the credit. This isn't easy. We wonder:

- ☺ What if I fail? How will God look then?
- ☺ What if He doesn't give me the power and I embarrass Him and myself?

You can counter this type of thinking by asking questions like:

- ☺ What if I don't fail?
- ☺ What if God does give me the power?
- ☺ What would happen if I don't ever try versus try and fail a few times before I get it right?

God wants to show His power in and through you! You can experience God at work when you choose to follow Him even when you feel insecure about yourself.

Embracing Hope

Let's add God's power to some things you might like to try. Imagine how tapping into His power might make things different in your life. In the space below, draw a picture to remind you to tap into God's power when you are feeling weak. Or write out a phrase you could use the next time you start to think things won't work.

....

....

....

....

Giving Your Sad to God

God, help me remember to tap into Your
power when I'm feeling weak. Amen.

24

STIRRING UP HAPPY

LYNN

"The heavens proclaim the glory of God. The skies display his craftsmanship."

Psalm 19:1 (NLT)

Laying back on my towel, a wide grin spread across my face. Basking in the warm sunshine, my heart felt light as I enjoyed the beauty of the summer day.

For me, there is something about getting outside that warms my insides. Whether I am going for a walk around the block in my neighborhood, hiking out in the middle of the woods, or traipsing in the snow, spending time in God's creation stirs up happiness in my heart.

I think nature did the same for David: "The heavens proclaim the glory of God. The skies display his craftsmanship." (Psalm 19:1) I can just picture him with his head bent back, looking up at the fluffy white clouds and thinking about how cool God is.

It's not just David and me who think nature makes us happy. Science tells us it is so! The air outside, the heat of the sun, the shade of trees; all of these things work together to make us feel better and make our bodies stronger!

So get outside! Even if it's cold, layer up and enjoy the

brisk air. If it's raining, grab a jacket and jump in a puddle. Give yourself the gift of God's creation and make some time to get out into nature!

Embracing Hope

Go outside! My coauthor Michelle calls it nature therapy. When you return, write on the lines below how you felt before you left, especially if you were inside for a while, and then how you felt when you returned from being outside.

....

....

....

....

Giving Your Sad to God

God, thank you so much for making such a big, beautiful world. In Jesus's name, Amen.

GO AHEAD AND CRY

LYNN

"I am weary with my crying; My throat is dry; My eyes fail while I wait for my God."

Psalm 69:3 (NKJV)

Sometimes when we are sad, what we need most is to cry; cry until we feel a bit better.

This is what Zoe needed when she received bad news.

The birthday party she went to was a blast! Now, it was time to go home. As she came through the front door, her mom called her to come back to her bedroom to talk. As they sat on the bed, her mom delivered devastating news: a friend from school had died in a plane crash. Her heart just could not take in that someone her age, just 11 years old, could die!

Zoe cried and cried. It was all she could do to get her emotions out and deal with such a big loss.

Zoe's mom sat beside her as she cried. Having her there when she was sad helped Zoe know her mom understood. Zoe didn't feel alone. She then called some friends and they also cried together, talking about how much they were going to miss their friend.

Talking about their grief together helped Zoe and her friends know their feelings were normal and they could help each other get through this very sad situation. This tragic event also helped Zoe learn that she could trust God to send people to help her in hard times.

Crying is actually a gift God gave us to help us process pain when we feel it. When we cry, our body releases chemicals that help us feel better. It helps us release tension and stress in our bodies.

So don't feel bad when you cry. Know that you are using an emotional gift God has given to us. And He is with you in your tears.

Embracing Hope

How do you feel about crying? Have you recognized its ability to help you feel better? Write on the lines below how you feel about crying. If you have a hard time releasing your tears, write out something you could say to yourself giving yourself permission to cry when you feel like it or need to.

....

....

....

....

Giving Your Sad to God

God, thank you for giving me the gift of crying. In Jesus's name, Amen.

SCARED— EMBRACING BRAVE

Meditation Matters

"Be strong and courageous. Do not be afraid or terrified because of them, for the LORD your God goes with you; he will never leave you nor forsake you."

DEUTERONOMY 31:6

"The LORD hears his people when they call to him for help. He rescues them from all their troubles."

PSALM 34:17 (NLT)

"When I am afraid, I put my trust in you."

PSALM 56:3

1

GOD WILL NEVER LEAVE YOU

MICHELLE

"Be strong and courageous. Do not be afraid or terrified because of them, for the Lᴏʀᴅ your God goes with you; he will never leave you nor forsake you."

Dᴇᴜᴛᴇʀᴏɴᴏᴍʏ 31:6

When my son was little, he developed a really big fear. His aunt and uncle were very sick and his cousins were worried they would both die. I spent a lot of time talking with his cousins and sister, who were older, about what was happening, but my son was very little and didn't talk a lot yet. He began to worry that both his dad and I might die and he would be all alone. That thought kept occurring and over time it grew into a GREAT BIG, SCARY FEAR. He didn't want us to leave him or him to leave us even to go to school. He didn't use his words to tell us what was happening. I'm not even sure he realized what was happening in his brain. Instead, his tummy would start hurting and he would often stay home sick or leave school in the middle of the day.

His stomach hurt so often that we took him to the doctor. She and I talked and as I took off my worried mom hat and put on my counselor hat, I realized he was struggling with something called separation anxiety and it was affecting him physically. We got some medicine to help him with the acid in his stomach. Then he and I went to work learning to calm his stomach down through belly breathing.

Belly breathing is when you take time to breathe deeply in through your nose and out through your mouth. You breathe so deeply that if you lay down flat and put a book on your tummy, you could move the book up and down. This type of breathing calms our entire body, including the pain we feel in our stomachs.

While my son worked on his belly breathing, we talked about how God was even a better parent than his dad or I could ever be. Believing in Jesus had made him part of God's family and he would always be God's son. While my son hopes his dad and I live a long time, he is learning that each day he can trust God. God is always with him and will be, even when the day comes that his dad and I are no longer on earth.

Embracing Brave

Practice belly breathing several times this week until you get good at it. You could lie on a couch with a book, spin a pinwheel by blowing on it, or blow bubbles by breathing deeply in and out. I like to think about breathing in God's love and breathing out my worries.

Giving Your Scared to God

God, thank you for promising to never leave or give up on me. Help me to breathe deeply when my body feels overwhelmed. Amen.

2

ALWAYS THINKING

LYNN

What are you thinking about right now?

Our minds are constantly thinking. Research says humans have about 60,000 thoughts per day. My mind can't even wrap around a number that big!

A lot of these thoughts begin small. It might look like this: *What is going on over there? I wonder . . .* Our thoughts appear random, flitting through our brains one after another. Yet some don't simply pass through. Without making a conscious choice, we choose to allow some thoughts to linger. When thoughts get stuck in our brains too long, we begin to focus on them and our thoughts create an emotion.

What is going on over there grows into *I'm scared of the unknown.* Fear begins to grow.

I've discovered a practice that helps me avoid heading in the direction of fear and I think it may work for you as well.

In between the first thought and the emotion that could grow, we can choose to reset our mindsets or redirect the thought in our mind toward a thought that feels better in our body. We can decide what our next thought will be and help our emotion shift to a positive place.

Isaiah 26:3 tells us: "You will keep in perfect peace all who trust in you, all whose thoughts are fixed on you!" (NLT) What a comforting place for our minds to focus on and what a promise from God; perfect peace when we trust in Him.

Embracing Brave

Practice fixing, or setting, your thoughts on God. Think about His love, His kindness, His power, and His goodness. In the space below write how you see God's love, kindness, power, and goodness in your life.

....

....

....

....

Giving Your Scared to God

God, setting my mind on You feels like work. It isn't easy.
Help me to keep making my thoughts more like the promises
and truths I find in Your Word. In Jesus's name, Amen.

3
MEET NEW PEOPLE WITH CONFIDENCE

MICHELLE

> *"Have I not commanded you? Be strong and courageous. Do not be afraid, do not be discouraged, for the LORD your God will be with you wherever you go."*
>
> JOSHUA 1:9

"Mom, I'm not sure I'll know anyone there," my daughter said as she prepared to leave for a church event. Sophia loves hanging out with her friends but gets a little nervous about being in a large group of people where she doesn't know anyone.

Have you ever felt like Sophia? Sometimes in order to experience some of the best things life has to offer, we have to feel our fear but not let it stop us. Often when we move forward despite our fears, it turns out that new wasn't as scary as we made it seem in our minds. I engage with lots of kids who tell me they have social anxiety, but as we talk they realize they really don't have a disorder. They are simply experiencing a typical reaction to the thought of going to a new place or being around people they don't know at all or not very well.

Recently, I was worrying about meeting someone for the first time—concerned about what she would think of me. A friend encouraged me to not worry but instead focus on the other person, ask them questions about their life and try to discover things we have in common. When we meet new people and focus on making them feel good about themselves, people relax, causing them to feel more confident. They, in turn, can enjoy being around us. The people we are meant to be friends with will connect with us because that is God's plan.

Embracing Brave

In your mind, create a movie scene of meeting someone new or going someplace you've never been. As you approach and interact with these people, take a deep breath. Imagine yourself thinking, "There you are." Thinking these three words helps you focus on showing interest in other people instead of worrying about yourself and what they are thinking about you. You may even want to think of three questions you can ask them.

Giving Your Scared to God

God, I know You are with me wherever I go. When I feel scared, help me focus on pleasing You and not others when I meet people for the first time. Help me to be friendly, but know that not everyone is meant to be my friend. Amen

TAKE MY WORRY

4

LYNN

> *"Don't worry about anything; instead, pray about everything. Tell God what you need, and thank him for all he has done. … His peace will guard your hearts and minds as you live in Christ Jesus."*
>
> PHILIPPIANS 4:6-7 (NLT)

"Can I go to a friend's house this weekend?"

"We'll see." That's the answer my husband often gave our kids when they would ask a question.

That answer drove them crazy! They wanted us to say yes right away so they could relax and know they were getting to go.

Having to wait for answers when we're uncertain of the outcome can cause us to feel scared.

Paul, one of Jesus's followers, had a lot of experience with outcomes that were not what he wanted. One of those experiences was being pushed around and bullied by people who didn't love Jesus.

From prison, Paul wrote: "Don't worry about anything; instead, pray about everything. Tell God what you need, and thank him for all he has done." Philippians 4:6 (NLT) You would think that being in prison meant he could no longer do the good work God had for him to do. It didn't! From prison, Paul wrote letters that are part of the Bible you and I read today. These letters Paul wrote help you and me today to know God better!

Let's take Paul's wisdom and direct our thoughts of uncertainty in a different direction. We can take the things we're concerned about to God. We can tell God our worries and trust Him to take care of things beyond our control.

And while this doesn't guarantee things will go exactly as we want, God does promise the peace of God will help our minds and bodies calm down no matter what our future holds.

Embracing Brave

Research says that writing out our troubles helps us give them to God. It gets those worries out of our heads. Writing them out can make us feel that we are bigger than our worry. On the lines below, write out your worries and then tell God you want Him to be your worry holder.

....

....

....

....

Giving Your Scared to God

God, thank you for taking my worries. Thank you for taking care of me when I worry. Help me to feel your peace. In Jesus's name, Amen.

GOD TO THE RESCUE

MICHELLE

"The LORD hears his people when they call to him for help. He rescues them from all their troubles."

PSALM 34:17

Have you ever done something and then knew you were going to get in trouble for it? Maybe it's not the first time you forgot to turn in your homework. Or you aren't even sure why, but you lied about something when you could have told the truth. Realizing we messed up and someone might be upset with us makes our hearts race, bodies sweat, and stomachs hurt.

In the Bible, Adam and Eve broke God's one rule and their first response was to hide from Him. But they couldn't hide, and neither can we. Hiding isn't even necessary because God already knows. Also, He wants us to turn to Him so we can experience His love even when we feel like we've failed. When we mess up big time, we can ask God for help.

The next time you feel scared, turn to God and ask Him for help. He may not change your situation, but He can and will rescue you from the overwhelming thoughts and feeling that makes you want to run, hide, or not even try.

Embracing Brave

Write down choices you've made that still cause you to feel bad inside. After you've made your list, color a big cross over them. If after doing so you keep struggling with a certain bad choice or sin, ask an adult for help. Some bad habits are harder to break than others, but with the help of God and people who know Him, you can do hard things!

....

....

....

....

Giving Your Scared to God

God, thank You that because of Jesus, You don't punish me when I mess up. Instead, You want me to let go of my past mistakes and walk in freedom because Jesus, through His death on the cross, forgives me and overcame sin for me. I am so thankful there is nothing I could ever do, and no trouble I could get in, from which You cannot rescue me. Amen.

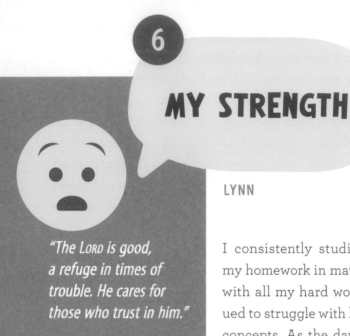

6

MY STRENGTH

LYNN

"The Lord is good, a refuge in times of trouble. He cares for those who trust in him."

Nahum 1:7

I consistently studied and did my homework in math. Yet, even with all my hard work, I continued to struggle with learning the concepts. As the day of the test got closer, my fear ramped up stronger and stronger. Though I had done all I knew to do, I still didn't feel confident I would make a good grade on the test. Now the test date was here.

While some people get a burst of energy when they take a test or play their instrument at a recital, others experience the opposite. It feels as though a boulder has been dropped on their chest or their thoughts become blurry. Even though they played the instrument great in their room by themselves, their fingers won't go where they're supposed to on the instrument now. Everything they've studied seems to disappear from their mind.

If you've experienced these feelings, you're not alone. Lots of kids struggle when they need to perform under pressure.

Nahum 1:7 is a great verse to rely on when we're reeling from pressure: "The LORD is good, a refuge in times of trouble.

He cares for those who trust in him." When we're afraid or feel trouble around us, we can feel weak.

God says when we're afraid, He will become our strength because He cares for those who trust Him. As His children, we are not helpless. He is with us and the Holy Spirit is in us. He will guard and protect us. Trusting God does not mean the things we fear, such as not performing well, will never happen. Choosing to trust God means even if things do not go the way we want, we can face what comes because God is by our side.

Embracing Brave

When fear is strong, if you have a hard time breathing, begin with the number 9 and count backward by 2, skipping every other number. 9, 7, 5, 3, 1. Using distraction by counting in an unusual way can help your heartrate settle.

Giving Your Scared to God

God, I can't make scary things go away, but I can come to You to be my strength, my defense, and my salvation in the middle of my fear. In Jesus's name, Amen.

OVERCOME FEAR AND ANXIETY

7

MICHELLE

"When I am afraid, I put my trust in you."

PSALM 56:3

"I have anxiety." When I meet kids and they find out I am a counselor, they often share things like this with me. I then become curious. Lately, I hear words like anxiety and depression more often. I wonder if you have heard a friend or someone at school use these words.

I asked one girl, "What does that mean?" She told me she often feels really nervous, and when she does, her stomach hurts. As a counselor, I want kids who might be experiencing anxiety to get help. And just like we teach kids in our offices, I want you to know that a diagnosis like anxiety is not something that stays with you forever. Just like other problems you would see a doctor for, it's something that can be treated and often gets better, goes away, or becomes manageable with a treatment plan.

Anxiety is created when we experience outside stress and inside worry and fear. Worry is like a dragon. You can either shrink it by turning to God and reminding yourself of His promises, or you can grow it by focusing on your worries all the time and letting them grow stronger in your mind.

Putting our trust in God sounds easy, but it takes practice for it to become a habit. It's kind of like brushing your teeth. If you only brush them every once in a while, you may need to figure out a way to remind yourself, which takes more energy. Trusting God is a decision we make because we choose Him to be the most important person in our lives. It's easier to choose God when we know Him. We can learn about Him from reading the Bible and talking with other people who know and trust Him. When we walk with God and practice trusting Him, He can help us be less afraid. I tell my kids I've never met a "worry dragon" bigger than God.

Embracing Brave

Write down one thing that scares you, worries you, or gives you anxiety. Now imagine God beside you. What would He say to you? What would He do? Imagine Him giving you the power to face your fear so that even if it's scary on the outside, you can be strong on the inside.

....

....

....

....

Giving Your Scared to God

God, I know You don't want me to live in fear. Help me feel brave when I am scared. Thank you that You are always by my side to help me face my fears. Amen.

I AM NOT!

LYNN

> "'You aren't one of this man's disciples too, are you?' she asked Peter. He replied, 'I am not.'"
>
> JOHN 18:17

Have you ever done something wrong and then because you were scared, lied to cover it up?

You're not the only one who's done that. I have and so did one of Jesus's best friends.

In John 13–16, Jesus told His friends a hard time was coming. He starts talking about this in John 13:36: "Jesus replied, "'Where I am going, you cannot follow now, but you will follow later.'" He continues explaining this to His disciples in chapters 14–16. He was going away and where He was going they couldn't come.

Then, just as Jesus said, frightening things began happening to Him. Men who wanted to harm Him came into a garden when He was praying and took Jesus away. The disciples were very frightened.

Peter, one of Jesus's disciples, followed to see what they would do to Jesus. When Peter arrived, there was a servant girl guarding the door. "'You aren't one of this man's disciples too, are you?'" she asked Peter. He replied, 'I am not.' (John 18:17)

Afraid of what might happen to him, Peter lied to try to

cover up that he was one of Jesus's followers. How sad Peter must have felt! I imagine he would have experienced regret, sorrow, and remorse for his actions.

He did two things wrong; not standing by Jesus *and* lying about their friendship.

Later, in John 21:15–19, Jesus and Peter have a conversation. Here, Jesus made it clear He loved Peter and they were still friends.

When you are scared, you may be tempted to lie. We can learn from Peter and Jesus's friendship that Jesus forgives us when we fail.

Embracing Brave

Jesus restored Peter, demonstrating His love for him. Jesus affirmed Peter the same number of times Peter had denied Him. One the lines below describe a time you were tempted to lie or did lie. Then write out words that remind you God still loves you and forgives you when you sin or choose to disobey Him.

....

....

....

....

Giving Your Scared to God

Jesus, I want to be brave and handle scary things with truth. I need Your help. In Jesus's name, Amen.

DELIVERED FROM ALL MY FEARS

MICHELLE

"I sought the LORD, and he answered me; he delivered me from all my fears."

PSALM 34:4

Have you ever met someone who seemed fearless? It seems like from the time we are babies, some kids are naturally brave and others timid. As they grow, many fears seem to fill their minds. Extreme fears are called phobias. When we encounter something we fear greatly, like being in a small space, high places, or some type of bug like a spider, our bodies can react like we are going to die even when we are completely safe. Our heart begins to race, we can feel hot and flushed, and we just want to flee from that feeling as fast as possible.

I often encourage kids who are struggling with fears or phobias to do a fear or worry dump. I often pray with them first so they start out feeling calm and safe. Then I have them write all the fears they have stored in their heads. We then rate each fear on their list from one to ten. Next, we bring God into the picture as we look at each fear because the power of God is stronger than any fear our brains encounter or create. He will deliver us from all our fears one by one if we turn to Him and trust His truth.

Embracing Brave

Let's work on creating a safe place in your mind you can visit when you need it. Think about a place where you feel calm and peaceful. For some people that's in nature. For me, it's the beach, but for my daughter, it's hiking on a nature trail in the mountains. It might even be in your room under a soft blanket, where you feel very cozy. Now take yourself there in your head and involve your five senses. While breathing in 1, 2, 3 and out 1, 2, 3, see yourself there. You might write or draw it out in the space below. Then add in what you hear, feel, smell, and maybe even taste. Add as much detail as possible as you continue to breathe. Feel all your muscles relax. I like to then add God into my picture, sensing His Spirit and feeling His peace.

. . . .

. . . .

. . . .

. . . .

Giving Your Scared to God

God, thank you for creating safe places I can go to in my mind anytime I need to. Help me remember to spend time with You and visit my safe place anytime I'm feeling scared or overwhelmed. Thank you that in time You can deliver me from all my fears. Help me claim this promise often. Amen.

10

BUT WHAT IF THEY'RE WRONG?

LYNN

"Even though I walk through the darkest valley, I will fear no evil, for you are with me; your rod and your staff, they comfort me."

Psalm 23:4

Life can feel hard when you don't get to make some decisions yourself. For example a parent signs you up to play a sport or take a summer class you're not sure about. It makes you uncomfortable, even scared.

What if I'm not any good? What if no one likes me? Sometimes being forced to try something new can make a person feel misunderstood, helpless, and alone.

Maybe you're going to summer camp or to your grandparents' for a whole week in the summer and you've never been away from home for that long. You're scared of what you've never done before.

There was a woman in God's Word named Rebekah. She had good reason to feel scared. Her brother and father made a huge decision for her. One day, they chose who she would marry. The very next day, Rebekah's family asked her to leave home and go to the man who would be her husband. Genesis 24:57–58 says, "Then they said, 'Let's call the young woman and ask her about it.' So they called Rebekah, and asked her, 'Will you go with this man?' 'I will go,' she said."

Rebekah agreed to go to Isaac, the man who would be her husband. She chose to trust God even though she wasn't sure what her future would be like.

It can be hard to trust, especially when the situation is scary.

There is One we can *always* trust, who loves us, always has our best in mind, and is with us. Psalm 23:4 tells us "Even though I walk through the darkest valley, I will fear no evil, for you are with me; your rod and your staff, they comfort me."

Whatever you're facing, God is with you. He can calm you, reassuring you that you're not helpless and alone. Let's trust Him when we face scary situations.

Embracing Brave

Say out loud, I trust in You, God. You are with me. You comfort me.

Giving Your Scared to God

Jesus, scary situations are a bit less scary knowing
You're with me. In Jesus's name, Amen.

THE CURE OF KIND WORDS

MICHELLE

> *"Anxiety weighs down the heart, but a kind word cheers it up."*
>
> Proverbs 12:25

Have you ever heard of the five love languages? Dr. Gary Chapman has defined five different ways love can be expressed or received. They are words of affirmation, quality time, receiving gifts, acts of service, and physical touch.

Words of affirmation or speaking kind words to someone can make a huge difference in a person's life. For people who value positive words spoken about or over them, it can free them from the kind of negativity that leads to low self-esteem. Sometimes we can get stuck thinking we aren't good enough. These thoughts can lead to feelings of worthlessness that lead to worrying others think badly of us. That kind of spiral thinking can make us want to give up on living the lives God created for us.

Have you ever had someone speak or write down kind words about you? Did it make you want to live a life worthy of those words? When I went to church camp as a kid, we each hung a sock with our names on it on a clothes line. Throughout the week, we wrote "warm fuzzies" about each other on pieces of paper and put them in the socks. At the end of the week, we took the socks home. Whenever I had a bad day that year, I read those notes. To this day I have a treasure chest where I keep thank you notes from friends, clients, and people who love me that I can read if I'm feeling like my work doesn't matter or I'm not worthy to do what God has called me to do.

Embracing Brave

Start a new trend of writing or saying kind words to the people you love. When you are encouraging them, you are being God's vessel. He might use your words to help them overcome the anxiety they are feeling and walk in confidence. You'll help them remember their gifts, character, and contributions to our world.

Giving Your Scared to God

Lord, help me to be a vessel of kind words to others, being used by You to create more light and freedom in what sometimes seems like a dark world. Help me soak up the words of blessing others have spoken over me so that the kind words that ultimately come from You will energize me to do Your work here on earth. Amen.

12

HELP

LYNN

"Hear my cry for help, my King and my God, for to you I pray."

PSALM 5:2

Where did she go? She was right here a minute ago!

I was only five years old and the mall felt big and unfamiliar when I became separated from my mom. I was terrified. How was I going to find her? While I was looking, would someone notice I was lost?

I remember my heart pounding. My body shaking. Fear flooding me.

There have been many times I have experienced the rush of fear; the unknown of what would happen next.

While crying out to God does not always fix the problem immediately, talking to Him when I'm afraid reminds me I am not alone. It helps take my focus off what I fear and look to the One who can help me. There have been many times I have experienced the rush of fear—the unknown of what might happen next—*even as an adult.*

Sometimes when I need His help and words won't come, I pray a single prayer: Help. That's all; simply help. One word is all I need. I know He hears.

Embracing Brave

You may think prayers need to be long and fancy, but they don't. Just like you might use only the word help to call out to a parent, help is the only word you need when crying out to God. He knows exactly the type of help you need. In the space below write the word HELP! big and bold. Mark this page and come back to it when you need the reminder that all you need to do is ask for help and it is yours.

Giving Your Scared to God

Father, thank you that when I cry out for help,
you answer me. In Jesus's name, Amen.

PERFECT PEACE

MICHELLE

"You will keep in perfect peace all who trust in you, all whose thoughts are fixed on you!"

Isaiah 26:3 (NLT)

Have you ever been up in the middle of the night feeling scared, overwhelmed, and anxious? You just really want to feel some peace so you can go back to sleep. Maybe you are worried about a test, a project due date, whether someone is or will get mad at you, or if something in the future will or won't happen. You might have had a bad dream that seems so real the fear stays with you even after you've been awake and told yourself it wasn't real. Your heart keeps pounding, your body so restless you feel like you can't stay in bed.

Struggling with sleep is a tricky thing that lots of kids encounter. If you're struggling to fall asleep, it's important to develop a before-you-go-to-bed routine so you can teach your body to know it's time to rest. This might include a checklist you do in the same order every night. Baths or showers, brushing teeth, putting on pajamas, reading your Bible or a devotional before bed, and listening to relaxing music may help. Some teens and adults use a sound machine like I did when my babies were little. It's good for blocking out noise and providing a soothing sound.

If you have thoughts racing through your head, you might want to keep a journal by your bed to write. Writing can help slow down the thoughts in your head. The Bible tells us that God does not sleep and He will watch over us through the night (Psalm 121:2-4). I remind my kids of this truth when they have bad dreams or they feel like something is in the room with them. I've taught them to say to the darkness, "Go away in Jesus's name" because Jesus called Himself the light of the world (John 8:12).

Embracing Brave

Take a look at your sleep habits. Do you need to improve your routine? Warming up your body before you go to sleep can trick it into being sleepy because as we fall asleep, our body temperature falls. Taking a warm bath or drinking something warm like a relaxing hot tea can help your body begin to get sleepy. Baths several times a week also reduce muscle tension in your body and help you relax. Finally, learn more about God's perfect peace as you read His word, talk with Him, and learn to trust Him more each day.

Giving Your Scared to God

Father, I need Your help on the nights I struggle to fall
or stay asleep. Help me sense Your presence that brings
peace. May I not only know in my head that I am safe but
feel it in my heart, as I rest trusting in You. Amen.

TURN THE LIGHT ON

LYNN

"Let your unfailing love surround us, Lord, for our hope is in you alone."

Psalm 33:22 (NLT)

When I was in middle school, I dreaded going to my bedroom at night. By day, I had the coolest room. It took up the top floor of our little home. When I was younger, I shared this unique bedroom with my two sisters. But they grew up and left home which meant I was left in this big bedroom alone.

In the day, the slanted ceiling created neat cubbies that held each of our beds. At night, these same walls felt like spaces where someone could hide. The dark surrounded me, making it hard for me to sleep. I would lay there with my eyes wide open until I simply couldn't keep them open any longer.

One thing that helped was light. Being surrounded by light helped me to not be surrounded by fear. Once I allowed myself to turn on a light, and tell myself that it was not silly or immature for choosing to turn on a light, it helped my anxiousness.

The Bible tells us in Psalm 33:22, "Let your unfailing love surround us, Lord, for our hope is in you alone." Even when you and I are surrounded by fear, we're also surrounded by

God's love. Even when we're in the middle of what we fear, we can remind ourselves that God and His great love surround us.

Embracing Brave

If you're afraid of the dark like I was, turn the light on. You don't have to be embarrassed or feel ashamed that you want to see at night. You can choose to get a small nightlight or they even make special light bulbs for the purpose of leaving on while you sleep. Whatever step you choose to take, remind yourself it is ok to do this.

Giving Your Scared to God

Father, thank You that Your light will always make the darkness go away. In Jesus's name, Amen.

15

GOD WILL PROTECT YOU

MICHELLE

"The LORD will keep you from all harm—he will watch over your life."

PSALM 121:7

Have you ever felt unsafe? I have worked with kids who have been bullied and didn't feel safe on the playground or even in school hallways. Feeling helpless can leave us not only feeling scared but it puts our bodies into a mode called hyperarousal. Our bodies and minds are constantly on alert for danger and can't be calm unless we know we are safe.

The verse for this devotion reminds us that God will be our protector, watching over our life. Yes, we live in a broken world and bad things can happen. But we can work with God to gain His wisdom and ask for help from trusted adults whose job it is to keep us safe. Kids often tell me they don't want to tattle and make things worse. It's hard to trust others. But wise adults can be like God's eyes watching over you. Teachers and principals can watch for the bullying, catching those involved without students being aware someone had told the adults what was occurring.

One time a girl was making fun of my daughter at school while on a playground surrounded by a group of friends. My daughter asked her why she was being mean. Immediately, several of her friends spoke up reminding the girl that they were all friends and needed to be nice to each other.

Choosing great friends God can use to protect you will help you experience a feeling of being safe when you are with them. Just because we turn to God for help doesn't mean we can't ask others for help. Sometimes God uses other people in our lives to be our protectors.

Embracing Brave

If you are being hurt by someone, tell an adult you can trust. It may seem like it gets harder before it gets better, but it's always better than handling it on your own. If you see someone being teased, embarrassed, or hurt, stand up for them with your words and get them help.

Giving Your Scared to God

God, thank You for being my protector. Help me learn to trust other people to help me when I feel unsafe. Help me to relax and enjoy my time at school rather than worry about possible problems. Amen.

16

ROOM REARRANGE

LYNN

> "Surely God is my salvation; I will trust and not be afraid. The LORD, the LORD himself, is my strength and my defense; he has become my salvation."
>
> ISAIAH 12:2

When I was in middle school I struggled with being afraid of the dark. I wasn't used to sleeping alone in the room I used to share with my sisters. I couldn't see the stairs that led up to my room; they were concealed by a half wall, blocking my view of anyone who might be coming up the stairs.

Sometimes, when the fear felt like more than I could take, I would slip down the stairs and crawl in bed with my little brother. There I felt safe.

Do you know what would have helped me feel safer in my room? Being able to see the door.

Sometimes simply rearranging your room with the bed facing the door can bring a sense of safety. We feel safer when we can see.

When you are feeling afraid, remember Isaiah 12:2, "Surely God is my salvation; I will trust and not be afraid. The LORD, the LORD himself, is my strength and my defense;

he has become my salvation." We turn our minds toward the Lord, and if it helps, turn our beds to face the door.

Embracing Brave

If you suffer from being afraid of the dark like I did, ask your parent/guardian if you could rearrange your room so that your bed faces the door. You just might be surprised at how this helps! You could even turn rearranging your room into fun, adding a new nightlight. You could frame today's verse as a new decoration to put on your wall to remind you that Father God is with you so you do not have to be afraid.

Giving Your Scared to God

God, thank You that You are always with me, even when I can't see in the dark. In Jesus's name, Amen.

GOD CAN CALM YOUR SOUL

MICHELLE

"When anxiety was great within me, your consolation brought me joy."

PSALM 94:19

Fear, worry, and anxiety are words I hear a lot these days. While these issues can produce physical symptoms like trembling, sweating, and nausea, most of the ways they build up in our bodies are unseen.

We may long to experience God comforting our souls, but in the busyness of school, activities, friends, chores, gaming, and entertainment, most kids I talk to spend very little time caring for their souls. Caring for our souls is a practice every human needs to make time for in order to manage the outside stress we face on a daily basis.

God wants to help us manage the stresses of life. He wants to comfort us, but it's important we give Him time to work on our souls. I try and set aside time on Sundays as the Sabbath. This is a time for me to focus on God and allow Him to work on my soul. I usually start my Sabbath by attending church. Then in the afternoon, I read or listen to a book that teaches me godly principles or life truths. I sometimes take a prayer walk or spend time with a Christian friend talking about how

God is working in our lives. Recently I began trying to be still and practice God's presence quietly (Psalm 46:10). I started by setting thirty seconds on a timer because being still doesn't come easily to me.

Embracing Brave

Plan some soul time into your week. I've listed many suggestions above. Allow your mind and soul to rest and fully focus on God. When your thoughts start to wander, don't get upset. Just bring your thoughts back to God's presence, His Word, and His peace. Our brains can have over 60,000 thoughts a day, so it may take some time to focus.

Giving Your Scared to God

Lord, I confess I haven't taken very good care of my soul and have not made time to fight my worries and let them go. Help me develop the routine of setting aside time so you can bring me the peace that passes human understanding (Philippians 4:7). Amen.

18

SONG OF THE NIGHT

LYNN

> *"You are my hiding place; you will protect me from trouble and surround me with songs of deliverance."*
>
> PSALM 32:7

Recently, I spotted my husband grabbing his earphones as we headed up to our room. It had been a particularly hard day and I knew exactly what he was doing.

On days when he's feeling anxious or overwhelmed, he listens to worship music to quiet his mind as he goes to sleep. The words, many from the Bible, help his mind shift from what is hard to what is good ... Jesus. To help myself fall asleep and sleep well, I wear a soft mask over my eyes every night. When I put my sleeping mask over my eyes, it tells my brain it's time to go to sleep. Each one of us can use unique ways to help bring calmness to our minds and bodies as we rest for the night.

I have friends who use noise machines or apps as a way of quieting their minds as they go to sleep. These devices play sounds like a fan, ocean waves, or the wind. The consistent sound drowns out other noises, helping them fall asleep.

In Psalm 32:7, David says He finds God to be his hiding place. When do we need a hiding place? When we're scared or in trouble. David says to God, "You are my hiding place; you will protect me from trouble and surround me with songs of deliverance." Not only is God David's place to hide, but he says that God "put songs in my heart because you have saved me" (CEV). There in the scary place, David sings songs that remind him God is with him, loves him, and protects him.

Embracing Brave

Create a playlist of songs reminding you of God's strength that you can play when you go to sleep. You could create a playlist of peaceful instrumental music or use a white noise app. Or you could purchase a noise machine to help you to sleep at night.

Giving Your Scared to God

God, thank You for being my hiding place. In Jesus's name, Amen.

19

TRUST GOD WITH YOUR FUTURE

MICHELLE

> "For I know the plans I have for you," declares the LORD, "plans to prosper you and not to harm you, plans to give you hope and a future."
>
> JEREMIAH 29:11

"You don't understand. If I don't do well on the test, then I won't get a good grade. If I don't get good grades, I won't get into a good college. If I don't get into a good college, then I won't have a good job, and if I don't have a good job, I won't be happy."

I can't tell you how many times I've heard this from a stressed student. Spending lots of time thinking about the future can create worry in our minds which can lead to stress showing up in our bodies and turning into anxiety. We were created to live in the present. God even called himself "I AM"—not "I was" or "I will be." Yes, having goals is important but ultimately the future is in God's hands (Proverbs 16:9). Learning to be fully in the present moment takes time and focus but it allows us to fully enjoy today as we trust God with our tomorrows.

Embracing Brave

For the next couple of days, work at trying to be fully present for at least a few minutes a day. If you are in a classroom, focus your eyes on what is happening around you. If the teacher is teaching, listen to her, fully focused on what she is saying. If you are talking with a friend, focus your ears fully on what he is saying and not what you are going to say next. If you are outside, smell the fresh air or feel the wind on your face. Take a deep breath and choose not to worry about tomorrow; instead, focus on the here and now. This practice is called mindfulness and can slow your heartrate and even help your muscles relax.

Giving Your Scared to God

Lord, I give you the worries I have about the future—about myself, my friends, and my family. I choose to live in the present with You, trusting You have good plan for my future. Amen.

20

ASK THE
QUESTION

LYNN

> *"As Jesus was sitting on the Mount of Olives, the disciples came to him privately. 'Tell us,' they said, 'when will this happen, and what will be the sign of your coming and the end of the age?'"*
>
> **MATTHEW 24:3**

Not having enough information can sometimes make me feel scared. When I'm in a situation and unsure what's happening or what might happen next, my mind tries to fill in the blanks with negative details instead of positive ones.

Creating a negative future in our mind is the perfect scenario for anxiety to begin.

A wise step we can take to keep from getting scared and anxious is asking questions.

Are you afraid of what will happen next? Ask someone who might have the answer.

Are you uncertain of what you need? Seek out the person who can tell you.

In the book of Matthew in the Bible, Jesus is spending time with His disciples, teaching them. They don't understand what He's saying about the future. Matthew 24:3 says, "As Jesus was sitting on the Mount of Olives, the disciples came to him privately. 'Tell us,' they said, 'when will this happen, and what will be the sign of your coming and the end of the age?'" The rest of Matthew 24 and all of Matthew 25 is Jesus talking to them, giving more information. He doesn't get mad or think the disciples lack intelligence or are worthless for asking. Instead, He patiently helps them to understand. God loves it when we turn to Him with our questions.

Embracing Brave

Is there something troubling you? Think of a question you can ask someone that may help to relieve your fears. Remember that Jesus is always with you and doesn't mind when you ask questions.

Giving Your Scared to God

Jesus, I know I won't always understand. Thank You for not thinking less of me when I ask questions. In Your name, Amen.

ONE DAY AT A TIME

MICHELLE

> "Therefore do not worry about tomorrow, for tomorrow will worry about itself. Each day has enough trouble of its own."
>
> MATTHEW 6:34

I'm a list maker. When I was in elementary school, I made a homework list, keeping my work in a separate folder. In middle school, teachers made us use planners where we wrote our assignments down. In high school, I used a notebook with a calendar, a to-do list, a prayer list, and sermon notes.

Writing things down and checking them off makes me feel good. This practice is even scientifically proven because when you check off something on your list, it releases a feel good chemical called dopamine in your brain.

When kids come into my office overwhelmed and stressed out, I have them write out a to-do list. When we try to tackle too many tasks at once, it short circuits our brains because our short term memory keeps only a few pieces of information active at a time. One way to overcome this is to rehearse or say over and over again what we are thinking, hoping we can remember it later. This process of rehearsing can lead to something called rumination. It's like chewing the same piece of food over and over again! Ruminating on what we need to do stresses us out and our Father doesn't want us to feel stressed out.

Embracing Brave

Make a list of all the things running through your mind. When they are written down, you don't have to keep remembering them. Instead, you can just look at your list. Then you can decide what's most important and choose to do one thing at a time.

....

....

....

....

Giving Your Scared to God

God, help me face the tasks I think take forever or that I don't enjoy. Help me to break the big ones into smaller pieces so I can manage them. Amen.

EVERYTHING

LYNN

"For I can do everything through Christ, who gives me strength."

PHILIPPIANS 4:13 (NLT)

As my son stood to take his karate test, I held up both hands, moving each finger one at a time, and mouthed to him silently: "For I can do everything through Christ, who gives me strength." Ten fingers. Ten words. I was hoping he'd remember he was not alone and it would help him through the test that felt scary.

This verse is often quoted to help when we have to do scary or hard things. But today, as I read this verse in Philippians 4, I wondered if maybe we've missed something.

Paul, the writer, is talking about scary things, but not necessarily things like passing a test. Instead, he's telling his friends how he's learned what to do when life is hard. He shares how he has experienced some situations that have been embarrassing and other situations that have been the absolute best! Paul had times when he didn't have enough of what he felt he needed and times when he had more than enough. In the end, he writes: "For I can do everything through Christ, who gives me strength."

There will be times in life when we may feel scared that we don't have everything we need. Paul encourages the people he's writing to, as well as us today, that even when we feel like we don't have enough, we can have confidence that Christ will give us strength in every situation.

No matter what type of "scary" you find yourself in, remind your heart and mind that Christ lives in you.

Embracing Brave

Put both hands up in the air. Now, push each finger forward, as though you are counting, and repeat with each finger movement: "I can do all things through Christ who strengthens me." These motions make it easy to memorize this verse.

Giving Your Scared to God

Jesus, thank You for this promise that I can do all things because You strengthen me. In Jesus's name, Amen.

FEARLESS

MICHELLE

> *"So we can say with confidence, 'The Lᴏʀᴅ is my helper, so I will have no fear. What can mere people do to me?'"*
>
> **Hᴇʙʀᴇᴡs 13:6 (NLT)**

Growing up, I was taught that if I worked hard to please others, I would make them happy. If I made teachers and coaches happy, they might choose me for certain jobs I wanted or give me special favors. As I got older, I believed if I wanted people to like me, I needed to make them happy. I became a people pleaser.

Even today, sometimes I still struggle when I feel someone is disappointed in me. But I am learning that making everyone happy is impossible and exhausting. I'm learning that I was created to make God happy—not people (Galatians 1:10). This idea of being a God pleaser instead of a people pleaser has brought so much freedom into my life.

Reminding ourselves how much God loves us and how important it is to please Him can help us when we struggle with people pleasing. God promises to be our helper when we face tough situations and have to say "no" to friends so we can say "yes" to God.

Embracing Brave

If you think a choice you are making might disappoint someone, take 24 hours to pray about it, if possible. Remind yourself
you aren't responsible for anyone's feelings but your own. You
are responsible to God to do the right thing. If you're not sure
what the right thing is, it can be helpful to talk it out with
someone wise and ask them to pray for you as you make your
decision.

Giving Your Scared to God

God, I want to say yes to You even when it's hard. I don't
like people being disappointed or unhappy with me, but I
want to honor You in all I do. Thank You for comforting me
when I feel upset even when I did the right thing. Amen.

YOU CARE FOR ME

LYNN

"Cast all your anxiety on him because he cares for you."

1 Peter 5:7

For many years, Emily has been part of a basketball team. She loved to play and dreamed of one day playing varsity.

Then a situation came up between Emily and her teammates. She felt pressure from her teammates to behave in a way that didn't line up with the relationship Emily had with God. Emily wanted to keep her friendship with her teammates and continue playing basketball with them, but in her heart it didn't feel possible to do that and stay true to her relationship with Jesus. She felt sad when she considered quitting basketball and losing the friendships, but she desired to follow the Lord more.

Emily asked the Lord to give her peace about this hard decision. He reminded her of 1 Peter 5:7. Reflecting on this verse and how Jesus cared for her comforted Emily.

Another source of comfort for Emily was talking with her mom. After talking it out, Emily concluded that she couldn't play a sport over following the Lord. She called her coach and told him her decision. He told her that no matter what her decision was, he would continue to support her.

Emily still felt sad that she was choosing to not play basketball with that team anymore; it was hard to see the team going forward without her. In fact, there were times when she felt doubt about her decision. When she felt doubt, she continued to pray and trusted God to lead her to happier times. After some time, Emily did in fact see that she made the right decision. God brought her new friends and happiness because she trusted him with her decisions and feelings.

I'm telling you this story about Emily because I hope that it helps you to be brave. Some of the decisions we make in life will be very hard. Just because it's the right decision, doesn't make it easy. When life is hard, we can feel sad. As we express this sadness to God we can trust Him to comfort us and help us to keep moving forward.

Embracing Brave

Have you felt sad and then experienced God's comfort? Remind yourself of this experience when you are feeling sad again.

Giving Your Scared to God

God, life can be hard. Thank You that I am not helpless.
You are always with me. In Jesus's name, Amen.

WHAT WILL I WEAR?

25

MICHELLE

"Therefore I tell you, do not worry about your life, what you will eat or drink; or about your body, what you will wear. Is not life more than food, and the body more than clothes? Look at the birds of the air; they do not sow or reap or store away in barns, and yet your heavenly Father feeds them. Are you not much more valuable than they?"

MATTHEW 6:25-26

Do you ever worry about having the "right" clothes to wear? My kids are on two different sides of the spectrum. My son owns five pairs of the same track pants and his only variety is the color of the athletic shirts he prefers. He wears clothes to be comfy. My daughter, on the other hand, loves going to secondhand shops and buying vintage clothes. She has enough to fill a closet *and* a clothing rack. She loves the good feeling when her brain releases dopamine with a new purchase or being creative with her appearance and outfits.

Scripture doesn't have a lot to say about how you manage your wardrobe, but it does talk about how much time you spend worrying about your appearance or how you look. Especially when it is spent to please other people. Jesus knew we could easily be tempted to become obsessed with spending lots of time being worried about looking a certain way to impress others instead of focusing on pleasing Him. As a counselor, I've met kids so obsessed with others liking the way they looked, they were hurting themselves.

God wants us to walk confidently as His children on this earth. He doesn't want our confidence to come from what we wear or what others think about our clothes but from knowing we were made by Him (Jeremiah 1:5).

Embracing Brave

If you spend a lot of time stressing out about what you are going to wear and worrying about your appearance, work on breaking that habit. Decide what you are going to focus on instead, each time you start thinking about how you look. You could think about how much God loves you, say your favorite Bible verse to yourself, or even think about moments when God blessed you beyond what you were expecting.

Giving Your Scared to God

God, when I am worried about not having the right clothes or frustrated that I can't get something I want, help me remember You will take care of my needs just like You do for the birds. Amen.

MAD-EMBRACING CALM

Meditation Matters

"My dear brothers and sisters, take note of this: Everyone should be quick to listen, slow to speak and slow to become angry."

JAMES 1:19

"Fools vent their anger, but the wise quietly hold it back."

PROVERBS 29:11 (NLT)

"In your anger do not sin: Do not let the sun go down while you are still angry."

EPHESIANS 4:26

"People with understanding control their anger; a hot temper shows great foolishness."

PROVERBS 14:29 (NLT)

1
SLOW TO BECOME ANGRY

MICHELLE

"My dear brothers and sisters, take note of this: Everyone should be quick to listen, slow to speak and slow to become angry."

JAMES 1:19

Have you ever seen a cartoon of a bomb? The longer the fuse is, the more time it takes for the bomb to explode.

Each of us has a fuse of sorts in our own lives. This fuse determines how quickly we get angry or if we simmer for a long time before anger boils over. We did not ask for the length of our fuses. All of us are born with different personalities.

I grew up with a parent who could get angry and scary really fast. As my siblings and I got older, we would get angry and fight with each other in ways that now make me sad.

Family anger can be contagious. When I counsel families regarding anger, I usually work with each family member in a session by themselves. Changing angry ways involves turning away from habits people have of blaming others for their anger. You have to own your own emotion because each person can only change themselves.

While we can't control the way God made us or how other people in our family behave, we can learn to control our anger. This process involves retraining our brains to make calm our first goal. Being calm becomes more important than being right or getting your way immediately. I know it's possible to rewire our brains not only because I've helped kids do so, but also because I have worked on this process myself. Just know, it takes practice.

Embracing Calm

You can calm the fight, flight, and freeze part of your brain. Spend a few moments several times a week breathing and saying calm words of love and truth to yourself when you find yourself getting upset and then mad on the inside.

Write down some calm phrases you want to try or that worked for you.

....

....

....

....

Giving Your Mad to God

Lord, I need Your help. It takes work to hold onto my calm. Help me train my brain and body to react calmly when I feel like I'm being wronged or attacked. Breathe Your calm into my mind, body, and soul. Amen.

TURN AROUND

LYNN

*"Turn your back on sin;
do something good.
Embrace peace—don't
let it get away!"*

Psalm 34:14 (MSG)

When I was in the 4th grade, Chad was the fastest kid in our class. When we played baseball, he often got us out before we even took off for the base! That meant he was always picked first when we chose teams in gym class.

Even though I knew Chad was better at sports than me, I still got angry when he was chosen first. What I didn't know then, I recognize today. What I was feeling was jealousy. More athletic than me, I felt Chad had an unfair advantage over the rest of us. *Why did he get to experience success and the rest of us didn't?*

While I never have been able to answer that question, I have learned letting jealousy simmer in my heart leads to anger. Allowing anger to linger leads me to a place where I do something I later regret, like saying mean words that hurt others.

I like to read the Psalms because David and the other psalm writers often talk about the same type of feelings I experience. In Psalm 34, David's in trouble. He has more than one person upset with him, and it isn't his fault. If anyone has a right to be mad, it's David. And yet, he recognizes that when he doesn't respond in the right way, his next step is trouble. He shares this wisdom: "Turn your back on sin; do something good. Embrace peace—don't let it get away!" (Psalm 34:14)

You and I can do the same when we feel anger. We can take a step in a positive direction, opposite of the way we are feeling, and do something good such as giving the person we're jealous of a compliment or kind word.

When we take big steps like these, it can turn anger around and helps us find the way to peace.

Embracing Calm

The quicker you recognize you're feeling angry, the quicker you can get out of the anxiousness anger creates. When you feel angry, try to think of a positive step you can take that would be the opposite of how you feel, such as giving the person you are jealous of a kind word or action. This can be the first step toward calm and finding the peace Jesus has for us.

Giving Your Mad to God

Jesus, help me when I feel anger to take a step in the opposite direction. I know You want me to experience Your peace. In Jesus's name, Amen.

3
IT FEELS LIKE BAD IS WINNING

MICHELLE

"Be still before the LORD and wait patiently for him; do not fret when people succeed in their ways, when they carry out their wicked schemes. Refrain from anger and turn from wrath; do not fret—it leads only to evil."

PSALM 37:7-8

Have you ever studied really hard then seen someone cheat and end up getting a better grade than you? When we see other kids breaking the rules and it seems like they are rewarded, we can become angry about how life seems unfair. If we let our anger consume us, it can erupt in unhealthy ways. We can become jealous, resentful, unkind, or begin to feel sorry for ourselves. Feeling sorry can lead to complaining and even giving up.

Psalm 37:7–8 tells us not to fret or worry about what others do or when they get something they don't really deserve. God wants us to turn to Him instead. It's hard but God wants us to let it go and keep our eyes focused on Him and ourselves instead of other people and what they are doing or not doing.

Waiting patiently for God is something I struggle to do. I wish I could just make it happen. If you are the type of person that likes to get lots of things done quickly, you may also struggle with waiting patiently. Learning to wait on God is an important skill because it helps us stay calm and learn to trust His timing which is truly perfect. What can you do while you wait? You can talk to Him and ask for what you want. You can also see if He's trying to prepare you in new ways. I often find in the waiting God works on my character, so that when the time is right I'm better able to handle what comes my way.

Embracing Calm

Create a "What to Do While Waiting on God" checklist. I have on mine: pray, ask friends to pray, talk with a friend or family member when I'm struggling, listen to worship music, go back and look in my journal for a time when I waited on Him before and then He answered, remind myself of prayers God has already answered, and go for a walk.

Giving Your Mad to God

Lord, it's hard not to be resentful when I see other kids succeed in areas where I struggle. Help me to keep my eyes trained on You and wait for Your timing, knowing Your plans for me are good (Jeremiah 29:11). Amen.

WHEN I WANT TO FIGHT BACK

4

LYNN

"Jesus said, "My kingdom is not of this world. If it were, my servants would fight to prevent my arrest by the Jewish leaders. But now my kingdom is from another place."

JOHN 18:36

Like a dart blasting out of a Nerf gun, the text I received made my heart want to pop. *How dare he?* I thought. He clearly misunderstood my actions! The long text he sent was filled with hurtful words and was making my heart race.

I'm sure there were times while Jesus was on the earth when His friends felt the same way. People made rude comments about Jesus, doubting He was God's son. These people said mean things about the disciples too.

When others are mean to us or treat us unfairly, there is something inside of us that can make us want to fight—fight with our fists and fight with our words too.

In John 18, Jesus is talking to the very people who were saying untrue things and treating Him horribly. Some people were making fun and even hitting Him.

Here is what I'm learning from Jesus: no matter how someone is treating me, I don't have to lose my temper. I can remember with confidence I am God's child. I don't have to fight. Jesus tells the bully, "My kingdom is not of this world. If it were, my servants would fight to prevent my arrest by the Jewish leaders. But now my kingdom is from another place" (John 18:36).

You and I have chosen to be Jesus's friends and His servants too. Just like the disciples, we can choose to not fight people who are against us. We can recognize and find comfort, knowing the kingdom we belong to is heaven. Heaven is our true home, where our Father God is preparing a place for us to be with Him one day.

Embracing Calm

Do you have a bully in your life, who makes you mad? You don't have to deal with this alone. Ask an adult to help you come up with a strategy for your next step.

Giving Your Mad to God

Jesus, please bring peace to my heart and wisdom for how to handle the bullies. In Jesus's name, Amen.

GODLY SELF-CONTROL

MICHELLE

"Fools vent their anger, but the wise quietly hold it back."

PROVERBS 29:11 (NLT)

"I couldn't help it. She made me so angry!" When I was a middle school counselor, I often heard these words or something similar. When someone hurts you, revenge is a natural first response. But not controlling yourself when angry can lead to trouble.

The Bible tells us to make every effort to have self-control (2 Peter 1:5-6). Self-control is listed as a fruit of the Spirit in the book of Galatians. You can turn to God to help you hold back your anger. When someone threatens us, it's normal to want to fight back.

When I was in high school, there was a girl who told me she wanted to fight me. I told her I wouldn't hit her back even if she hit me. At first, she tried to get me to fight but when she realized I was serious, she called me "stupid" and walked away mad. I left and went home as quickly as I could.

Not all stories end like mine. I know kids who have been hurt by another when they wouldn't fight. Following God's ways can seem almost impossible in situations like these. But learning to be wise and trust God while holding your anger in for the moment can be one of the wisest moves you will make.

Embracing Calm

If you tend to get angry easily, first talk to God about the situation and ask Him to help you not blow up. Next, you might want to talk to someone you trust about your feelings and that relationship, and get some suggestions on how to handle that person in your life.

It's important that after we have held back our anger, we find ways to let the built-up energy in our bodies out. To release mine, I used to hit a tennis ball as hard as I could. Some people I know run out their mad. During the pandemic, my husband hung punching bags from a tree in our backyard to give him a way to release his energy.

Giving Your Mad to God

Lord, I confess I tend to want to let my anger explode when I'm mad. It's hard to hold it in. Help me take a time out, cool off, and then find a better way to solve my problems. Amen.

6

CHOOSE THEM

LYNN

> *"Don't be selfish; don't try to impress others. Be humble, thinking of others as better than yourselves. Don't look out only for your interests, but take an interest in others, too."*
>
> PHILIPPIANS 2:3-4 (NLT)

In elementary school, I loved to play on the monkey bars. One day, although I had asked my friend to play on the monkey bars during recess, as soon as we headed outside, he took off for the kickball field. *Didn't he hear me? Didn't he remember that I said I wanted us to play on the monkey bars?*

Furious, I stormed over to the monkey bars alone and began to swing round and round. But the fun I thought I would have didn't happen. I was too mad at my friend.

That day, I didn't ask my friend what he wanted to do during recess. I only thought about myself. And when he didn't do what I wanted, I became angry.

In Philippians, Paul writes a letter to his friends who also love Jesus and tells them, "Don't be selfish; don't try to impress others. Be humble, thinking of others than yourselves. Don't look out only for your interests, but take an interest in others, too."

Choosing to think of others stops my thoughts and actions when they are racing toward anger. Because I care about my friend or family member, I can ask about and pay attention to what they are interested in. I can ask how they might be feeling. Asking these questions can stop anger from leading me down a path I'll regret, where I not only feel angry inside, but I also say unkind things to others.

Choosing to think of others instead of myself can be very hard! We so often think of ourselves first. But if we ask the Holy Spirit to help us consider others and how *they* feel, he can empower us to be unselfish and love others well.

Embracing Calm

When you choose to spend time with someone today, ask where *they* want to go, what they want to eat, or what they want to do. Then choose that.

Giving Your Mad to God

Holy Spirit, help me to pay attention to what other people are interested in and not just what I want. In Jesus's name, Amen.

GET ALONG WITH ALMOST EVERYONE

MICHELLE

"If it is possible, as far as it depends on you, live at peace with everyone."

ROMANS 12:18

The first time I heard a teaching about Romans 12:18 I felt relief! Finally, I understood that we all have different personalities. This means some people might really get on my nerves and I might get on the nerves of others.

Living at peace with everyone doesn't mean you have to be friends with every person you meet. You can, however, be friendly. You can smile, be polite, and still choose not to spend tons of time with them.

While keeping your distance from someone seems like a great way to manage differences and avoid conflict, it's not always possible. You might be placed at a table in school or assigned to a group project with someone who annoys you.

Separating the person from their behaviors is a first step to getting along with someone who gets on your nerves. Next you might ask God to help you see them as He does. You might challenge yourself to think of at least one good thing about that person. (I bet you can find it if you try.) You can also remind yourself that you aren't with them all the time and even sitting close or working with them will come to an end. Remind yourself that with God, interacting kindly with someone who you don't like is possible (Matthew 19:26).

Embracing Calm

Close your eyes and see the face of someone who gets on your nerves and then bring God into the picture. The Bible says He loves them and created them for a purpose. Listen to what God says about them and ask Him to help you see good in them.

Giving Your Mad to God

God, help me to love people like You do, including those who seem unlovable to me. Amen.

8
I WISH YOU UNDERSTOOD

LYNN

> *"For we do not have a high priest who is unable to empathize with our weaknesses, but we have one who has been tempted in every way, just as we are—yet he did not sin."*
>
> HEBREWS 4:15

You just don't understand! My daughter shared her frustrated feelings and I sensed she was ready to blow up. I've felt this same way at times. When we think someone is not understanding how we feel, it can leave us feeling mad, sad, alone, and isolated.

If that is where we stop, hopeless in our emotions and with the sense that we're completely alone, we can find ourselves endlessly spinning.

While it's true no one can completely get you because they *aren't* you, here is some encouragement that's also true: Your Creator can and does understand, even your maddest of mad feelings. He gets you when you want to make someone else hurt as you hurt. He understands when you don't get why they said what they said and did what they did and you want to make them pay. Yes, He understands when you want to do something that is not right.

Hebrews 4:15 explains it this way: "For we do not have a high priest who is unable to empathize with our weaknesses, but we have one who has been tempted in every way, just as we are—yet he did not sin." Jesus isn't up in heaven wondering what your problem is. Since He came to earth as a human, He has experienced everything we experience. He felt anger. He experienced sadness. He can help us to feel the full weight of our feelings and still do the right thing. He's right here; ready to help. Let's ask Him to!

Embracing Calm

Take a moment and breathe in through your nose and out through your mouth filling your belly with air. As you breathe in, say in your mind, "You are with me." Breathe out, saying, "You are with me." Do this as many times as it takes for your heart to stop racing and for you to feel in control of yourself again.

Giving Your Mad to God

Jesus, thank You for coming to earth and going through hard things. It helps to know *someone* gets me and that the someone is You! Help me, with my strong emotions, to do the right thing. In Jesus's name, Amen.

9

GOD AS THE ULTIMATE AVENGER

MICHELLE

> *"Do not take revenge, my dear friends, but leave room for God's wrath, for it is written: 'It is mine to avenge; I will repay,' says the Lord."*
>
> ROMANS 12:19

"Watch out, he'll get you back!" I often warn my kids when they come up with tricks to play on their dad. Their father is a master trickster and whatever they do, he will come up with something ten times more devious. While playing tricks in our home can be fun, even this type of fun can turn into tears and anger if taken too far.

When someone says or does something mean, it's human to want to get them back. God's Word, however, asks us to leave our need for justice in God's hands. I find that hard to do sometimes because I know God forgives. But it helps me to remember He has often forgiven me for wrong thoughts and wrong choices I've made.

When someone says something mean to you, talks about you behind your back, or makes fun of you, you may be tempted to return their unkindness with unkindness of your own. Instead you might want to remind yourself that our true battles aren't with other people but are spiritual (Ephesians

6:12). Fighting human battles with spiritual power means letting God be our avenger and praying to Him for the strength to trust Him.

Embracing Calm

Is there someone you're angry with? Maybe it's a brother or sister and you want your parents to punish them. The Bible tells us to love and pray for our enemies (Matthew 5:44). If there are people you are mad at, pray for them. You might want to talk to God about them, writing on the lines below.

....

....

....

....

Giving Your Mad to God

God, it's hard to let go of wanting (fill in the blank) to be punished for what they've done to me. Help me to let go of the resentment I feel in my heart and trust You to handle them. Amen.

10

WITHOUT LOSING MY COOL

LYNN

"Control your temper, for anger labels you a fool."

Ecclesiastes 7:9 (NLT)

After heading up to the teacher's desk, I tried to get back to my chair as fast as possible. I was hoping no one would notice that I was struggling with my work... again.

Slipping quickly into my seat, I miscalculated where the chair was. Suddenly I found myself sitting on the floor. While my bottom burned from hitting the floor, it was nothing compared to my ketchup-red face. Instead of going unnoticed, I had done just the opposite. Everyone was staring at me and I could hear a snicker or two. Knowing they were talking about me made me feel embarrassed and that embarrassment quickly turned to anger. Why did they have to be so mean?

Though I felt angry, you know what mattered right then? What I would do *while* I was mad.

It's normal to feel mad when we're embarrassed. What can we do when we're mad so we don't act like a fool as Ecclesiastes 7:9 says?

With the Lord's help, we can control our emotions even when they want to control us. Ecclesiastes 7:9 (MSG) says it this way: "Don't be quick to fly off the handle. Anger boomerangs. You can spot a fool by the lumps on his head."

When we sense anger rising, with God's help, we can take a moment before we do something that brings us more embarrassment or even hurts someone.

Embracing Calm

Choose a place in your home to call your Control Corner; a space where you can get away from an embarrassing situation or go when you feel anger rising. Go here when you need some time and room to allow your anger to cool. Tell Jesus how you feel and ask Him for the self-control you need. It may help to write out these feelings in the space below.

....

....

....

....

Giving Your Mad to God

Jesus, I don't like feeling embarrassed, but I know it's going to happen. Help me learn self-control so I can handle these situations as they come, without losing my cool. In Your name, Amen.

11 WHEN YOU ARE MAD AT YOURSELF

MICHELLE

> "Therefore, there is now no condemnation for those who are in Christ Jesus."
>
> ROMANS 8:1

I have never met a human who hasn't made a mistake. Some mistakes are little and easy to let go. But for the kids I work with who struggle with perfectionism, letting go of mistakes can be really hard. Sometimes they get mad at themselves and become angry and stuck.

Mistakes can often lead to guilt or feeling bad about what you've done. But as someone who has put your faith in Christ, your guilt was erased over 2,000 years ago. And this includes all the mistakes you've ever made and all the mistakes you will make in the future. When God looks at you, He sees you through the filter of Jesus, which covers your sins and bad choices.

My daughter once made a really bad mistake and hid it from us for weeks. During that time, I noticed a change in her spirit. She seemed withdrawn and didn't have joy. I thought it was due to her broken leg. I was mistaken. Hiding her guilt from us led to shame and feeling bad about who she was.

When my daughter finally told us the truth, I could see she immediately felt better. She thought what she had done was so bad, we wouldn't love her anymore if we knew. But just like Jesus, we embraced her and while we didn't like what the choice she made cost us, we assured her there was nothing she could ever do that would change our love for her.

Embracing Calm

Make a list of any mistakes that are making you feel bad about yourself. Rip that list into tiny pieces and place them in a trash can. As you choose to let go of your past, thank Jesus for your freedom. Ask Him to help you live free, knowing your life will be messy. No longer thinking about the bad of your past, frees you to live happy today and hopeful for tomorrow.

Giving Your Mad to God

God, thank you for loving all of me. Help me to see myself as you see me, through the filter of Jesus. Help me to let go of the guilt of past mistakes so I can enjoy today. Amen.

12

GOD, FORGIVE ME

LYNN

"Have mercy on me, O God, because of your unfailing love. Because of your great compassion, blot out the stain of my sins. Wash me clean from my guilt. Purify me from my sin."

PSALM 51:1-2 (NLT)

Why did I say that ugly thing to my friend? She was my closest friend; the one who knew all of my secrets. Yet sometimes, she makes me angrier than anyone else can. And when that happens, sometimes I say mean, hurtful things to her.

I felt hurt and I hurt her back. Then I felt horrible and guilty.

Sometimes, because we're human, we fail. We feel the strong emotion of anger and in the middle of that anger, we do what's wrong. That's called sin.

Once we've done what we shouldn't, what do we do next?

We ask God to forgive us; we ask Him to take away our sin and make our heart clean again.

In Psalm 51:1-2, David, king of Israel, blew it. He did what he shouldn't have. David sees his own wrongdoing and instead of doing another wrong thing, like hiding or denying it, he admits his sin to God. He asks God to have mercy, to be compassionate, and not give him the punishment he deserves.

He knows God loves him and is kind. He asks God to make him clean again. And God did because He promises that when we ask for forgiveness, He'll give it! (1 John 1:9)

Embracing Calm

Sometimes when we sin, we pretend or even say we didn't. (Which is the sin of lying.) It takes maturity to admit we've done wrong; both to the person we've wronged and to the Lord. Because you're becoming mature, the next time you sin, be brave, asking both the person you've wronged and the Lord for forgiveness.

Giving Your Mad to God

Father, help me be brave and humble, not proud, when I do wrong. Give me the courage to ask for forgiveness each time. In Jesus's name, Amen.

YOU CAN BE ANGRY

MICHELLE

"In your anger do not sin: Do not let the sun go down while you are still angry."

Ephesians 4:26

When the Bible says not to let the sun go down while you're angry, I don't think it means we should keep arguing and fighting with each other until someone gives up. I believe this passage means we are to avoid bitterness and being so mad our emotions seem stuck in our heart and body.

Something I learned when visiting a church recovery program, a small group meeting where people get help for their problems, is HALT. HALT stands for Hungry, Angry, Lonely, and Tired. People who teach HALT say it's a good idea to stop talking with someone if you notice you are hungry, angry, lonely, or tired. When we are not at our best, our brains stop working correctly and we may say and do things we don't mean.

Embracing Calm

The next time you find yourself feeling really mad, try practicing the solutions for HALT. Go get something to eat, practice some of the calm-down skills you've learned in this book like breathing deeply and distracting your mind, talk it out with someone you trust, or chill out for a small period of time—if possible, take a nap.

Giving Your Mad to God

God, when I am starting to get mad, help me check to see if I'm hungry, angry, lonely, or tired so I can be calm when I interact with others. Amen.

14

ARE YOU MAD?

LYNN

"But you desire honesty from the womb, teaching me wisdom even there."

PSALM 51:6 (NLT)

When I was young, I began a habit that's been hard to break.

When someone would ask if I was mad, I would say "no" even if I was.

Though I don't know *when* I started lying about this, I do know *why* I did it. I didn't want someone to be angry at me for being mad. Does that sound silly?

Maybe it doesn't because you struggle with the same thing.

If we believe being mad is bad, we might start lying about the way we feel. We don't want to be mad *and* bad!

But you know what?

It's not bad to be mad, but it is wrong to lie.

In Psalm 51, David is talking to God about something he's done wrong. He knows he's chosen wrong and in the first two verses of this psalm, David asks God to forgive him. In verse 6, David says to God, ". . . you delight in truth in the inward being" (ESV). David recognizes God wants us to be honest; honest with Him and honest with other people.

I know it can be scary to be honest. I struggle with that too! If we choose to be brave and are truthful about how we feel, it can lift heaviness off our hearts. Hopefully, it will also open an opportunity for you to share with others how you really feel, allowing room for healing and growth in your life.

Embracing Calm

Being honest takes practice. Try it out first on small things like when someone asks you what you'd like for a snack or what you want to watch on TV. Tell them what you want and begin to get strong in being honest. On the lines below, write a list of things you want to start being more honest about.

....

....

....

....

Giving Your Mad to God

Jesus, I want to always be honest. I need
your power. In Jesus's name, Amen.

15

FLEE FROM RAGE

MICHELLE

"Get rid of all bitterness, rage and anger, brawling and slander, along with every form of malice."

EPHESIANS 4:31

Rage is scary! When someone has lost control of their anger, they may yell, say mean things, threaten to hurt someone, throw things, punch holes in walls, or even hurt someone's body.

When I work with families who have rage inside their homes, we come up with a plan to stop right away. We make an agreement that if anyone in the house feels like they are going to start raging, they have to walk away and the other person needs to let them go. No one may talk until everyone involved is completely calm. If the people in the house can't control themselves and it's unsafe, sometimes people have to live apart for a while. While someone leaving a home is hard and sad, it's a better choice than someone in the family getting hurt.

You may be reading the words above thinking your house doesn't have any rage in it. Thank God if you live in a peaceful home and ask Him to help you be a good listener if a friend ever shares about their angry home struggles. Ask God to continue creating in you a desire to respond peacefully when your parents say "no" to your request to do something you want to do or buy something that you think you really need.

Embracing Calm

Talk to one of the adults in your house about practicing time-outs when anyone in the house is really mad and starting to lose control.

Giving Your Mad to God

God, help me to ask for a timeout any time my heart starts racing and I am tempted to say or do something wrong in my moment of mad. Help me practice good ways to calm down so when I talk with others, I can be kind instead of cruel. Amen.

16

WHEN I FEEL LIKE GIVING IN

LYNN

> *"But the fruit of the Spirit is love, joy, peace, forbearance, kindness, goodness, faithfulness, gentleness, and self-control. Against such things, there is no law."*
>
> **GALATIANS 5:22-23**

You know when you're so upset it seems like you'll explode? Yeah, me too!

At times like these, it feels like there is nothing we can do when we're furious. We feel out of control; like we can't stop whatever we might say or do.

I've learned a secret though: the Holy Spirit can empower us to control our actions even when our emotions feel like they're controlling us. The word for this is *self-control*.

The Bible tells us in Galatians 5:22–23 that self-control is a sign that the Holy Spirit is working *in* us. It's important for us to understand what it means for the Holy Spirit to be in us. In John 14, Jesus is preparing His disciples for the time when He will return to heaven to be with His Father. Jesus is reassuring His friends that although He will physically not be with them anymore, He is leaving those who love Him with a great gift: his Holy Spirit. The reason this is so great is that no matter where we are or what is happening in our lives, the Holy Spirit is in us, helping us. When we allow the Holy Spirit's power to work in our lives, we see beautiful things in us. The Bible calls these traits the "fruit of the Spirit" (Galatians 5:22). Think of it like apples on an apple tree. Since it is an apple tree, it grows apples. Since you and I are followers of Jesus, we grow love, joy, peace, forbearance, kindness, goodness, faithfulness, gentleness, and self-control.

Yes, because the Holy Spirit lives inside those of us who have chosen Jesus, as we ask, He will teach us how to have self-control and direct our energies wisely, even when that energy feels negative.

Embracing Calm

Reread Galatians 5:22–23 at the beginning of this devotion to review the list of the traits the Holy Spirit works into our lives. This "fruit" comes from having the Spirit in you, not from you being perfect. Take a moment to recognize that to have self-control, you're going to need power from the Holy Spirit.

Giving Your Mad to God

Jesus, controlling myself is hard! Thank you for sending your Spirit to live in me, helping me do hard things. In Jesus's name, Amen.

ANGER CONTROL

MICHELLE

People with understanding control their anger; a hot temper shows great foolishness.

PROVERBS 14:29 (NLT)

"I'm mad. I'm really, really mad." As my preschooler told me how he felt about having to pick up his toys and stop playing, I smiled at his words, because he was naming his emotions.

One of the first steps to releasing your emotions is to name them. Say the name to yourself or out loud. Then try and figure out where you feel the mad in your body. Is your heart racing? Does your stomach hurt? Maybe there is a place in your body that tenses up, like your neck or shoulders.

If you feel you are getting angry a lot, you may need to adjust or change your expectations about what you want to happen next. The reason my son was so mad was he expected to play with his toys as long as he wanted and resented being interrupted by me.

As I write these words, Nolan is now almost twelve, but his biggest struggle with anger today is very similar to when he was three. Now he plays games online with his friends. He makes plans without always checking our family schedule.

So when I ask him to do something or tell him we have to go somewhere, I can see him battling his anger about things not going his way and choosing to control how loud his voice is, how distressed he sounds, and the words he chooses to use. I think about when he first started working on responding calmly. I could tell by watching his face and body, it was a hard struggle. But over time and with practice, it seemed to take less time for him to control his emotions.

Embracing Calm

Sometimes when I work with families in our counseling offices, parents report to me that their child is mad all the time but often the kid doesn't agree. I then ask everyone in the family to track when they got mad for a week. I ask them to write down what happened and then rate on a scale from one to ten how mad they got. If you struggle with melting down and getting mad, you might want to check the frequency (how often your mad happens) and intensity (how big it is on a scale from one to ten).

Giving Your Mad to God

God, help me train my brain to become more flexible instead of getting mad when my plans are interrupted. Amen.

PUT ON LOVE

LYNN

> "Therefore, as God's chosen people, holy and dearly loved, clothe yourselves with compassion, kindness, humility, gentleness and patience."
>
> COLOSSIANS 3:12

Take a second to think about what you chose to wear today.

This morning, I made my way to the closet looking for something cozy. I wanted something comfortable. Grabbing my favorite sweatpants, I slid them on.

I chose to put on sweatpants because that is what I wanted to wear.

Paul, in his letter to his friends, told them to intentionally put on something too. He told them in Colossians 3:12: "Therefore, as God's chosen people, holy and dearly loved, clothe yourselves with compassion, kindness, humility, gentleness and patience."

When we purposefully choose to be tender, kind, humble, gentle, and patient, we send a signal to our brains that this is the way, as God's child, we're going to live.

Making this choice is not easy! But if we make this choice over and over, we will develop a habit. When we find ourselves in situations when we want to react in anger and we choose to have self-control, we are training our brain that this is the way it's going to be.

Embracing Calm

What did you choose to wear today? Just as you chose what to wear, you can choose how you'll react when you are mad. It won't be easy, but with God's help and practice, it will become easier. On the lines below, write about one character trait you will choose to wear today.

....

....

....

....

Giving Your Mad to God

Jesus, help me choose compassion, kindness, humility, gentleness, and patience even when I feel angry. In Jesus's name, Amen.

JEALOUS MUCH?

MICHELLE

"Anger is cruel, and wrath is like a flood, but jealousy is even more dangerous."

Proverbs 27:4 (NLT)

Jealousy makes us miserable. In a world where we are often compared to a brother or sister, another student, or even a friend, we sometimes feel like we are competing against everyone and everything. We find ourselves continuously wanting to be as good as someone else or wishing we could have what they have.

God loves us all, but He doesn't make us all the same. Wouldn't that be boring if He did? Each one of us has our own strengths and weakness. Often when we are jealous of someone, we are focusing only on their strengths and our weaknesses.

As a writer and speaker, jealousy is a temptation I often face. If I spend too much time looking around at what other people are doing, I can become discouraged. I even sometimes get mad at God because I wish I had the chance to write on a certain topic or go speak in a certain part of the country. I'm grateful God helps me in those times by reminding me to stay in my own lane so I can win my own race. When I focus on my race and the reasons God made me, plus thank Him for His blessings, it becomes much easier to stop my longing to be like someone else. Gratitude is a great cure for jealousy.

Embracing Calm

The next time you are mad or jealous of someone, you might try practicing wants versus needs. For example, a newer smartphone is a luxury (an extra big blessing we don't need but would make our life fun) not a necessity (something we need to live).

Giving Your Mad to God

God, help my brain to spend more time focused on what I have already been given, rather than what I want. I confess I take a lot of my blessings for granted. Thank you for all the blessings I've already received. Bless me so I can be a blessing to others like it says in Genesis 12. Amen.

WHO'S THE UMPIRE?

LYNN

"Let the peace of Christ rule in your hearts, since as members of one body you were called to peace. And be thankful."

COLOSSIANS 3:15

Do you play sports or watch a family member play? Most of the time there will be an umpire or referee. This is the person behind the plate or running up and down the court, watching what's happening. They call someone out if they have too many strikes. They take a player out of the game if they aren't a good sport. These people call the shots in the game and have a lot of power.

The word *rule* in Colossians 3:15 means "to act as umpire." Paul, who wrote this letter to his friends, said to let the peace that comes from Jesus rule or act as the umpire in their lives. He doesn't want them to let anger, sadness, fear, or any other emotion control them and call the shots in their lives. Instead, he says, "Let the peace of Christ rule in your hearts."

How do we do that?

Paul tells them in Colossians 3:14 to "put on love." (ESV)

Before you play soccer, baseball, or other games, you put on a uniform. Paul tells us that even more important than putting on a uniform, we need to put on love because love will help us to have peace and friendship with others.

Purposing in our hearts to put on love and to act in peace and friendship with other people helps us when we feel mad. We can learn to stop before we act and choose peace instead of allowing anger to control us.

Embracing Calm

Sometimes we get angriest with those we love most. When you feel mad at your parent, sibling, or closest friend, journal your feelings so you get them out. Then remind yourself of this person's love so the love covers the mad. Hopefully you know they love you. You know they want the best for you. Let this truth calm your heart before you act.

Giving Your Mad to God:

Holy Spirit, give me the power I need to have Your peace, instead of anger. Rule my heart. In Jesus's name, Amen.

COVER THEM WITH KINDNESS

MICHELLE

"Be kind and compassionate to one another, forgiving each other, just as in Christ God forgave you."

Ephesians 4:32

Have you ever met someone you thought didn't like you at first, but after spending time together, you became really good friends?

In college, I took a Greek language class where we studied the New Testament words as they were actually written. A girl named Michelle (We have the same first name!) and I were the only girls in class. She sat by a guy named Jeff who at the time was her boyfriend and is now her husband. I thought since we were the only girls, over time we would be friends. When I smiled at her though, I felt like she never smiled back. Later we talked about this and she told me she never noticed me smiling at her.

During the second semester I groaned inwardly when she sat down beside me in chapel because I thought she didn't like me. Being the talker that I am, I couldn't keep myself from sharing a comment with her. She laughed at whatever I said and that small exchange of words began what is now a 30-year friendship.

Recently, something difficult happened in the life of someone with whom I have a hard time getting along. I kept sensing God wanted me to give the person a gift I only give special friends. I kept asking, "Are You sure, God?" and even asked one of my close Christian friends if she thought I was crazy. She encouraged me to listen to what God was telling me to do and obey Him even if it didn't make sense to me. I was worried how the person would react and shared this with God. I realized it wasn't my job to control her response but to act in obedience. She barely responded but in my heart something changed. When I hear or think about her, I don't have strong feelings of resentment anymore. I am able to practice letting go of my hurt a little more with each act of kindness.

Embracing Calm

Choose someone you think doesn't like you or that you've gotten mad at and be kind to them. It could be as simple as sharing a smile or giving a small gift to them. No matter how they respond, know that you are following God's plan for your life.

Giving Your Mad to God

God, please show me if there is anyone in my life whom You'd like me to share a gift or perform an act of kindness for. I want to spread Your love to others—even those I feel don't like me or have hurt or rejected me. Help to me to act in faith, trusting You. Amen.

NOTHING IS HIDDEN

LYNN

"You, God, know my folly; my guilt is not hidden from you."

PSALM 69:5

My stomach hurt, not from what I ate, but from what I had done. I was feeling guilty for the way I acted when I had gotten so mad at my sister.

Even though I asked her to forgive me, I still felt rotten inside.

If we lose self-control when we're angry and act in a way that is wrong, the bad feelings add a layer on top of our anger. The whole situation becomes one huge mess.

At times like these, we need to go to God, just like David did in the Psalms. We tell God we know we messed up, which is called confessing our sin. We admit that we can't hide what we've done and we need His forgiveness.

When we do this, God promises us He will forgive us, and wash us to be "whiter than snow" (Psalm 51:7). Knowing we are forgiven can help us feel happy again.

Embracing Calm

If it is winter and you live in a place where there is snow on the ground, go outside and find a patch of snow that has no dirt on it. If this isn't possible, do an internet search with the words: beautiful, white snow. How would you describe the clean snow? How does seeing this snow make you feel? Our hearts can feel clean when we know Jesus has forgiven us for what we've done wrong. Write the answers on these lines below.

....

....

....

....

Giving Your Mad to God

Jesus, I know how I have messed up. Please forgive me. In Jesus's name, Amen.

23

AVOID ANGRY FRIENDS

MICHELLE

"Do not make friends with a hot-tempered person, do not associate with one easily angered."

PROVERBS 22:24

"Fight! Fight! Fight!" I could hear the group chanting as the principal and I raced down the hallway. When I was a middle school counselor, I spent a lot of time talking with girls about repairing friendships, calling a truce, or clearing up miscommunication when one girl threatened another. These conflicts often started when one girl talked behind the back of another. This caused feelings of betrayal. Instead of helping these girls clear up the situation, their friends would often go back and forth between the two, sometimes even setting up a plan to fight or encouraging them to take revenge.

Planning to physically fight with someone is not a good idea. In our offices, we teach kids hands are not for hitting and hurting, but for helping and hugging. Sometimes we make a friend when we're young, but as we become older, the friendship doesn't remain a healthy one. Then we need to make a decision to spend less time around that person.

Embracing Calm

Take a sheet of paper and make a list of your current friends, starting with the ones to whom you are closest and moving toward the ones with whom you don't spend as much time. Next, beside each name write out some of their strengths and weaknesses. You might have an adult help you print out a list of character traits to give you a variety of words from which you can choose. Words like generous, kind, loyal, funny, smart, great listener, fun to play with, caring, and good at protecting your privacy are examples of positive character traits. Words like jealous, bossy, angry, foolish, and sarcastic are examples of negative character traits. Make a promise to yourself to spend more time with the friends who have positive traits.

If you look at your friend list and think it's too small, it might be just fine. Research says we can only really have a couple of close friends and then only a half dozen or so good friends. If you've recently moved or your list seems too short, ask God to bring to mind anyone whom you've met that you'd like to spend more time with who has positive traits.

Giving Your Mad to God

Lord, help me find and keep close friends who help me feel positive about myself and encourage me to follow You. Help me to stay friendly and spend most of my time around those who love You and Your ways. Amen.

FLEX THAT MUSCLE

LYNN

UGH!

I tried *everything*, trying to get my iPad connected to the internet. Nothing worked. I felt like exploding; frustration growing stronger and stronger. I needed to get my work done. *What was I going to do?*

I bet you've had a similar problem a time or two. No matter what you do, it doesn't make a difference. You're on the verge of screaming, giving up, or both.

When we're not experiencing success, we can feel disappointed, angry, and not smart enough.

I've discovered that being able to keep going even when I'm frustrated is kind of like working my muscles. When I first started doing push-ups, I could only do a couple. But the more I kept trying, even when frustrated, the stronger I became.

The same can be true with strengthening our muscles of patience and perseverance. As we practice patience and perseverance, we grow stronger and can tolerate frustration longer, developing new levels of strength.

Embracing Calm

When we're frustrated, we can stop what we're doing and acknowledge, "I am very frustrated right now." Sometimes, just saying what we feel can help us feel calmer and release our frustration.

We can breathe deeply, asking the Holy Spirit to help us. Then exhale, picturing ourselves blowing out the frustration. After exhaling, we can try to figure out our next step. It may mean stepping away to regain self-control. Sometimes, as we think of what we've tried so far, a new idea may come to mind. If we are feeling embarrassed, perhaps we need to overcome it and ask for help, so we can move forward like our verse today: "Finishing is better than starting. Patience is better than pride" (Ecclesiastes 7:8 NLT).

Giving Your Mad to God

Holy Spirit, give me Your power to grow strong in handling frustration. In Jesus's name, Amen.

HANG ON FOR A BIT

LYNN

I typed a text back as fast as I could. I couldn't believe my friend had said that to me! Her words were so mean. After hitting send I felt better.

When she didn't respond, though, I started wondering about what I had said. I read the text again. Yes, she had been mean to me, but I was mean right back. I did the same thing I was mad about! Now I wished I hadn't sent it.

That is the tough thing about texts and spoken words too. Once they are out, there is no taking them back.

I had done the opposite of Psalm 4:4, "Don't sin by letting anger control you. Think about it overnight and remain silent . . ." I let anger control me and sinned by being unkind. I wish I had slowed down, thought about it, prayed, and asked God for wisdom. I should have waited overnight to figure out the right thing to do.

You and I can learn to slow down when we get angry so that we don't do things we later regret. That is very hard to do on our own; sometimes it feels impossible! But with the power of the Holy Spirit living in us and by learning the tools of self-control, we avoid situations when we have to say, "I wish I hadn't done that!"

Embracing Calm

When you feel upset, count backward from 10 to 1, giving yourself time to calm down. After you are done counting, try to determine if you need more time. Waiting a day or two before talking to the person we are frustrated with can also prevent us from creating more problems with a friend.

Giving Your Mad to God

Holy Spirit, it doesn't come naturally for me to wait to do or say something when I'm mad. Give me Your power and help me learn to slow down before I do something I'll regret. In Jesus's name, Amen.

HAPPY-EMBRACING JOY

Meditation Matters

"Surely goodness and mercy shall follow me all the days of my life: and I will dwell In the house of the Lord forever."

Psalm 23:6

"Delight yourself in the Lord, and he will give you the desires of your heart."

Psalm 37:4 (ESV)

"Rejoice in the Lord always; again I will say, rejoice."

Philippians 4:4 (ESV)

"Rejoice always, pray without ceasing, give thanks in all circumstances; for this is the will of God in Christ Jesus for you."

1 Thessalonians 5:16-18 (ESV)

HOLDING ONTO HAPPY

MICHELLE

> *"Surely goodness and mercy shall follow me all the days of my life; and I will dwell in the house of the Lord Forever."*
>
> **Psalm 23:6 (NKJV)**

If you could write a script of your future, what would it contain? Let's take a moment to believe in God's goodness and dream of what our futures could hold.

I remember doing this in middle school and again in high school. Between those two times, my hopes and vision changed. When I was in middle school, I saw myself with long blond hair, smiling and wearing suits like lawyers wear in court. I envisioned myself living in a fancy apartment and driving a nice car.

By the time I was in high school, God had changed the vision of my future as I spent more time seeking Him. There was nothing wrong with my middle school dream, but my high school dream of becoming a mental health professional and a minister was the perfect fit for how God created me. I followed that dream, and I am so happy doing these things with my life.

While I love my life and work, the last part of Psalm 23:6 makes me most excited. Sometimes life here on earth is amazing! Other times it's really difficult. But something I can count on for sure is one day I will spend every moment living in God's house—heaven. I can't wait for that time when I no longer have to worry about the pressure I feel living on earth. One day I will receive the gift of leaving behind the troubles of this world and the struggles with my human mind, body, and heart, and exchange them for a new body and spend eternity with God. I'm not even sure what that will be like, but living in God's house forever sounds like a pretty good deal.

Embracing Joy

When you think about your future, make a choice to see it as one filled with blessings from God.

Slow down and take a moment to picture this in your mind. Should any fear try to creep in as you picture your future, tell it to leave. You can train your mind to believe God has great plans for you (Jeremiah 29:11) not only for today, but also for tomorrow and the years ahead.

Sharing Your Happy with God

God, I am excited to see how Your goodness and mercy will shape my future here on earth. Thank you that at the end of that time I can count on the promise of being with You forever. Amen.

SO GOOD

LYNN

> *"Taste and see that the Lord is good; blessed is the one who takes refuge in him."*
>
> Psalm 34:8

The summer before I began attending a new school, I worried. I wondered how I would make friends. Would I meet some kids who liked what I liked? Kids I would have things in common with? Then I met Wanda that summer.

Wanda went to my new school. She asked me if I liked to run. Run? I had never really thought about running. I ran when I played basketball or went around bases in softball. I even ran after the ball in volleyball. But run just to run? Nope.

Wanda said she was part of a running team at school. It was open to anyone who wanted to join. That sounded like a good way to meet friends. So in the middle of the hot summer, I started running. I was slow but by the time school started, I could run two miles without stopping. In my diary, I wrote: "Running is a lot of fun." I tried something new and found I liked it; I discovered running was good.

The same can be true in our relationship with Jesus. If we begin a relationship with Him, or as David, the writer of Psalm

34, said, "taste and see," we will find the Lord is good. He is a wonderful God and savior. Jesus can be our best friend.

Embracing Joy

Ask a friend, sibling, or parent about a food they like that you have never tried and write those in the lines below. Now make a choice—try them! Taste and see. Is it good? Think about how good it can be to try new things and the happiness we might find when we do.

....

....

....

....

Sharing Your Happy with God

Jesus, I don't have to guess whether or not You are good.
I already know you are! In Jesus's name, Amen.

3

DELIGHTING IN THE LORD

MICHELLE

> *"Delight yourself in the*
> *Lord, and he will give you*
> *the desires of your heart."*
>
> **Psalm 37:4 (ESV)**

"Mom, I'm so happy I can't stand it," my daughter said as I entered the room.

"Wow!" I said. "What are you celebrating?"

"Coraline 2 is coming out."

Knowing that Coraline was her favorite movie, I laughed and then replied, "Well, if that makes you happy, I'm happy for you."

What delights or makes your soul happy? Some kids feel amazing when they do well in a sport or on a test. Some get excited when they make a new friend or get invited to someone's birthday party. Others celebrate big time when school is out for the summer or they're on vacation. I remember wanting a certain present for my birthday or Christmas, and I thought if I got it, I'd be truly happy. Funny thing is I don't own any of those presents anymore.

God gives us blessings and wants to celebrate them with us. But He also wants us to learn a life skill that will keep us in a happy zone even when things don't go our way: He asks us to find joy in Him. Not in what He does or gives us, but just in who He is. He's a God who made us and loves us. He is all-powerful and knows everything, and the Bible says He's for us.

When we learn more about Him through reading the Bible, and spend time with Him in prayer and worship, we learn to line our desires up with His will. We can get excited when we learn something new in the Bible, hear a song about Him that makes us happy, or He helps us when we pray. When we line up our thinking and what we care about with what God cares about, our hearts want what He wants. When that happens, something supernatural occurs. We receive the desires of our hearts because we don't just want things here on earth, but we care about things that last forever.

Embracing Joy

Take a sheet of paper and divide it in half. On one side make a list of what the world says will make us happy. On the other, make a list of what God's Word says will make us happy forever. If you aren't sure what would be on God's side, ask a grown up or Christian friend for help. Your God list doesn't need to be long. In fact, I pray it will grow as you move toward becoming an adult. Hopefully even then, you will keep learning about God's desires for us.

Sharing Your Happy with God

God, it's so easy to get caught up and distracted with things on earth that make us happy for a minute. Help us discover the desires of Your heart, so we will be happy for a lifetime. Amen.

COME ON IN!

4

LYNN

"Enter his gates with thanksgiving and his courts with praise; give thanks to him and praise his name."

PSALM 100:4

In elementary school, I was part of a choir. One of the songs we sang was Psalm 100 put to music. (I love when Scripture is put to music because it's so easy to memorize!)

This psalm begins: "Shout for joy to the LORD, all the earth. Worship the LORD with gladness; come before him with joyful songs" (vv. 1–2). Sometimes, before I get out of bed in the morning, I will go over these words in my head. *Shout for joy to the Lord!* (It would be even better if I shouted them, wouldn't it? That might frighten my sleeping family though!) I've found that when I think of Scripture, it automatically points my heart to "happy." It's like I'm giving my heart and mind directions for the way we're going today; the direction is toward happiness.

The writer of this psalm goes on to give us the reason for being happy: "Know that the LORD is God. It is he who made us, and we are his; we are his people, the sheep of his pasture" (v. 3). We are happy because we belong to God! He made us

166

and He made us wonderfully. Every day, He guides us on the way to go.

The next couple of sentences tell me exactly how to start my day: "Enter his gates with thanksgiving and his courts with praise; give thanks to him and praise his name" (v. 4). When we begin our day being thankful, telling God how wonderful He is, our heart cannot help but be happy! Thankfulness directs our hearts and minds to be happy.

The writer ends by giving us words to use when we are telling God how great He is: "For the LORD is good and his love endures forever; his faithfulness continues through all generations" (v. 5). The Lord is good. His love for us is never-ending; never stopping.

Embracing Joy

If you can, go outside and shout out loud: "The Lord is good! His love endures forever!"

Sharing Your Happy with God

Jesus, thank You that You are faithful. Thank you for being good and always doing what You say You will. Your promises are a good reason to be happy. In Jesus's name, Amen.

5

JOY NO MATTER WHAT

MICHELLE

"The Lord is my strength and my shield; my heart trusts in him, and he helps me. My heart leaps for joy, and with my song I praise him."

PSALM 28:7

What makes your heart leap for joy? Let's take a moment and dwell on times you've been really happy. Moments I remember are getting my cat Beauty as a kitten, making a best friend right after moving, making the tennis team, and being chosen as Miss Peppy of the Year in a middle school pep rally. I can also remember the first time a boy liked me back. It's important to spend time thinking about the good times in our lives. It helps balance out our brains for when times are tough or we are experiencing the more uncomfortable feelings of mad, sad, and scared.

Did you know God wants you to trust in Him no matter the circumstances and where our feelings take us? We live in a broken world. It is the opposite of heaven, so sometimes we hurt a lot. But we can turn to God; He will be our help. He doesn't always fix what's broken, but He often protects our minds and hearts from feeling too much. He holds us tight, reminding us that things will get better. When times are good, celebrate hard. I like to scream a little, shout a little, and dance a lot. Your ways of being happy may be quieter, and that's okay. What's important is spending time dwelling on the good.

Embracing Joy

On a separate sheet of paper, draw a road representing a timeline of your life. Mark some good things that have happened along the way. You might want to place it where you can see it often, reminding yourself of the good things. Leave some space to add more good things as they happen down the road. When you are finished, you might want to turn on some happy or worship music and dance to show your joy. Dancing releases all kinds of good things in your body and makes your happy even greater.

Sharing Your Happy with God

God, thank You that I can trust You in good times and bad. Help me train my brain when I'm thinking about my life, to learn from the hard and then leave it behind, focusing on the good. Amen.

6
WHY I AM BLESSED

LYNN

> *"Blessed is the people of whom this is true; blessed is the people whose God is the LORD."*
>
> **PSALM 144:15**

Are there words that people use at church, but you don't quite understand? Me too! One of those words is *blessed*.

I looked up *blessed* in the dictionary so I could understand this verse: "Blessed is the people of whom this is true; blessed is the people whose God is the LORD" (Psalm 144:15).

God is my Lord, so what is *blessed*?

Blessed has several meanings, but the one I thought best matched this verse is: *blissfully happy or contented*.

Why would those who know and follow God be full of joy?

In the verses before this one, the writer of the Psalm gives us many reasons for being so full of joy:

- ☺ God is dependable. (Psalm 144:1)
- ☺ God's love is stubborn in helping us. (Psalm 144:2)
- ☺ God is my safe place. (Psalm 144:2)
- ☺ God is my protection. (Psalm 144:2)

Those are very good reasons for us to be happy; happy to be His!

Embracing Joy

As you are learning that God is someone who will be dependable, who you can count on as a safe place and for protection, how might that make you feel happy?

....

....

....

....

Sharing Your Happy with God

Jesus, thank You for being all these things and more for me. I am happy and grateful that You're in my life! In Jesus's name, Amen.

7

JOY IN GOD'S PRESENCE

MICHELLE

> *"You will show me the way of life, granting me the joy of your presence and the pleasures of living with you forever."*
>
> PSALM 16:11 (NLT)

My daughter Sophia has loved singing worship songs since she was a little girl. I remember her singing in her car seat when she was in preschool. Now she's in high school and she loves leading worship at church. Using YouTube, she taught herself to play the keyboard, electric guitar, and acoustic guitar. This summer she started teaching herself the ukulele. Sophia has found listening to and singing worship songs to God makes her aware of His presence and brings her joy. I can see it on her face as she sings or listens to the radio in the car on the way to school.

Finding songs that remind you of times of joy you experienced when worshiping God is a great way to tap into His presence anytime. In our house, we play a recording of God's Word or our favorite worship songs. Many of these songs are about heaven and being with Jesus forever, which is so encouraging on days when it's been tough here on earth. The thought of living with Jesus forever comforts me.

Embracing Joy

Are there songs you sing at church or hear on the radio that remind you of God's presence and the joy we can find in Him? One song that I've loved for a long time is called "There is Joy in the Lord" by Cheri Keaggy. Make a list of a few songs that bring you into the joy of God's presence. With your parent's help or permission make a playlist so you can play them when you're feeling down.

....

....

....

....

Sharing Your Happy with God

God, thanks for creating music that reminds me of your presence and brings me joy even when I'm not in the best mood. Amen.

BECAUSE I TRUST YOU

LYNN

> *"Whoever gives heed to instruction prospers, and blessed is the one who trusts in the LORD."*
>
> **PROVERBS 16:20**

As my family watched the movers put the last piece of furniture on the moving truck, my heart was sad. I didn't want to move. I loved our town and our friends.

Piling into our car, I began telling the Lord, "I trust you." I told God that even though I was sad, I trusted that He had good things ahead for me and our family.

The first year in our new town was hard. Making new friends and finding the way around a new school doesn't happen overnight.

When I look back now, I am very happy we moved. Proverbs 16:20 is true, "Whoever gives heed to instruction prospers and blessed is the one who trusts in the LORD." My family sensed the move we were making was the move God wanted us to make, and we were right! We now lived closer to family and then found a wonderful church and friends. We trusted the Lord and had been blessed. I'm glad we trusted Him when we felt so sad in the middle of our move.

You will have experiences in your life when you won't understand why something is happening. You'll feel unsure. In the middle of hard places, we can reach out to our Father and ask Him to help us trust Him. Trusting God over and over leads to joy. Trusting in God instead of our own abilities takes the pressure off us and puts it on Jesus. Jesus can handle anything and helps us find joy even in difficult situations.

Embracing Joy

Can you think of a time when you felt sad, but things turned out and you were happy? Write about such a time. Come back and read your story again the next time you need to trust Jesus with your future. Remembering times like these helps us trust God and find joy in our future.

....

....

....

.. ..

Sharing Your Happy with God

Jesus, thank you for every time I have trusted you. Trusting You brings joy to my life. In Jesus's name, Amen.

9
GIVING OTHERS WHAT THEY NEED

LYNN

"Now may the God of hope fill you with all joy and peace as you believe in Him so that you may overflow with hope by the power of the Holy Spirit."

ROMANS 15:13 (HCSB)

Following Jesus and doing life His way can be a lot different from what I feel like doing or even what seems normal. I'm also finding living life His way often leads me to be happy.

In the book of Romans, Paul, one of Jesus's followers, says: "Now may the God of hope fill you with all joy and peace as you believe in Him so that you may overflow with hope by the power of the Holy Spirit." I find it interesting when a verse begins with the word *now*. It's a clue that the verses before help explain what I am about to read.

If we go back and read Romans 15:1–12, we find out what Paul said before he said *now*. He told Jesus's followers how they should be treating each other. Paul says as Jesus's followers we should be patient with those who are not as strong as us. God's strength in us makes us want to be kind to others. He encourages us to be patient by finding strength in God, and to show others how good God is by the way we treat them.

Paul tells us to be patient, kind, and loving toward others. God promises us joy and peace as a result of this. He tells us that the hope *we* need can overflow to us when we look to the Holy Spirit to fill us.

When I think about God's promises, I am filled with joy because I know that what I need—patience, kindness, and love—and what I want—joy—all come from loving and serving our good God. I know that as you love and serve Him, you too will experience His joy and peace.

Embracing Joy

Who in your life needs you to be patient, kind, and loving toward them? Trust that as you ask God to give you what you need to do this, He will fill you with happiness. On the lines below, write a prayer asking God to give you what you need to be kind toward that someone in your life.

....

....

....

....

Sharing Your Happy with God

Jesus, giving others what they need can help me receive the joy and peace I need from You. Fill me with your patience, kindness, and love so I can share it with others. In Your name, Amen.

10

JOY IN THE HOLY SPIRIT

MICHELLE

"For the kingdom of God is not a matter of eating and drinking, but of righteousness, peace and joy in the Holy Spirit."

ROMANS 14:17

What does it mean to have joy in the Holy Spirit? Before we tackle the entire phrase maybe we should think about what joy means. I think joy is a feeling that comes from being connected to God and expecting His goodness to follow you (Psalm 23:6). Joy might seem illogical because it is not based on what we are currently experiencing in our lives. Joy is a positive feeling we experience in our hearts as we think about God and heaven even when life is not so good here on earth.

For people who don't know God, joy might not make a lot of sense. But feeling joy doesn't mean we ignore feelings like sadness, anger, and fear. After we feel them, we filter what's happening in our lives by including God and holding onto His promises. When we connect with God and remind ourselves of His love for us and His promises for our lives, we can feel joyful even when life is hard. Our joy comes from changing what our mind is focusing on.

Deep down in my heart I know God is with me and for me, but when bad things happen, I sometimes doubt what I know to be true. It's like I'm wrestling inside. I call this the battle of the mind. Galatians 5:16–18 calls it the conflict between the flesh and spirit (earthly experience verses heavenly perspective).

Embracing Joy

Think about some situations when you have reacted using only your logical mind, excluding your spiritual wisdom. Now add God's perspective into the picture, integrating your human thoughts and your Spirit-led mind. How does this change what you think and feel about the situation? Practicing using your Spirit-led mind as you think through typical situations in life can prepare you to keep joy in the Holy Spirit when you are tempted to only focus on what you experience in the moment.

Sharing Your Happy with God

God, help me to be led by Your Spirit and not just focus
on what's happening in the moment. Amen.

THINK ON THIS

LYNN

"And now, dear brothers and sisters, one final thing. Fix your thoughts on what is true, and honorable, and right, and pure, and lovely, and admirable. Think about things that are excellent and worthy of praise."

PHILIPPIANS 4:8 (NLT)

When I think about the things that make me happy, they seem to fit into categories. For instance, the fact that my family loves me. That fits into the "what is true" category. I have my needs met and some of my wants too. This is in the "what is right" category. My friends and family take care of me and I take care of them. These are honorable and excellent.

I know, every day, without a doubt, my heavenly Father loves me and is rooting for me. Knowing I have worth because of Jesus fills my heart with joy because there is nothing that can ever take away what God has given to me. Even if I go through a hard season when I don't have everything I feel I need or have troubles in my family, the love God keeps sending my way never changes.

It is good for us, as Paul told his friends the Philippians, to focus on what is good. We can keep reminding ourselves of all we have to be happy for. Focusing on the good is also called practicing gratitude. Practicing gratitude reminds us of all the things we have that make us happy.

Embracing Joy

On the lines below and on a small piece of paper or sticky note, write out this verse—Philippians 4:8 (NLT). Put this paper where you look often, such as the corner of your computer or on the mirror in your bathroom. For the next week, read it at least once a day and at the end of the week see if you can say it without looking at it.

. . . .

. . . .

. . . .

. . . .

Sharing Your Happy with God

Father, help me focus my thoughts on what is true, honorable, right, pure, lovely, and admirable. In Jesus's name, Amen.

12

FILLED WITH JOY

MICHELLE

"But let the godly rejoice. Let them be in God's presence. Let them be filled with joy."

PSALM 68:3 (NLT)

What brings you joy? Because you are uniquely made, every one of us has a different answer to this question. You might find joy in the taste of a great meal. Someone else could care less what they eat. You might find joy in building muscles, making them stronger and bigger. That might not sound fun to someone else.

One thing that brings me a lot of joy lately is lighting a candle or two. Some people call this aromatherapy. When I smell certain scents and hear the crackle that comes from a new candle I received as a gift, it fills my heart with joy.

We can learn more about how we were made to experience joy by trying different things and observing how we feel when we do them. As we trust in God, we discover how He made us so we can be reflections of Him. He created us to be made in His image (James 3:9).

When I experience joy from life's simple pleasures, I thank God for creating them and gifting them to me. Recognizing God as the ultimate source of joy increases our trust in Him.

As we intentionally create moments that bring us joy, our joy overflows to others. I love bringing the hope and joy of God into my counseling office and praying with my clients. As I read Psalm 68:3, it inspires me to pray that as you read this devotion, you will be filled with joy and peace as you learn to trust in God more each day of your life.

Embracing Joy

Make a list of ten simple things you have control over that bring you joy. Do at least two of these every day this week to increase the joy in your life.

....

....

....

....

Sharing Your Happy with God

Father, help me discover things that bring me
joy and to do them often. Amen.

HOLDING ON TO HAPPY

LYNN

"I have told you these things so that you will be filled with my joy. Yes, your joy will overflow!"

JOHN 15:11 (NLT)

I know you've had it happen before. Your day has been going amazingly well; one good thing after another. You're laughing. You're happy. Life is so much fun!

When suddenly . . . bam!

Something goes wrong and all the good feelings come to a halt. Now you're feeling everything *but* happy.

Do you know it is possible to not have your happiness stolen from you?

In John 15:11, Jesus is talking to His friends, sharing with them the secret to hanging on to happiness. "I have told you these things so that you will be filled with my joy. Yes, your joy will overflow!"

What did Jesus tell them would fill them with joy? So much joy it's spilling over?

He said: "I have loved you even as the Father has loved me. Remain in my love." (John 15:9 NLT) That's the secret— understanding how much Father God and Jesus love us! Knowing how much He loves us causes our hearts to feel full.

We know that we can never be unlovable. It's not possible!
When we experience tough times that steal our joy, we know
God will fill us up with His joy again and again.

Embracing Joy

Draw a picture in the space below of things that make you
happy. Be sure to draw something to represent the love of
Jesus.

....

....

....

....

Sharing Your Happy with God

Jesus, thank you that Your love makes me happy when
I have things going perfectly as well as when they're
not going so great. In Jesus's name, Amen.

JOY IN YOUR WORK

MICHELLE

"You will enjoy the fruit of your labor. How joyful and prosperous you will be!"

PSALM 128:2 (NLT)

Do you like to work? Work is a strange concept. What can seem like work to one person is fun for someone else. For example, I don't really like to clean. I have a brain that easily gets overwhelmed when I have to do too many things at once. But I have a friend who loves to clean. It relaxes her. Cleaning is work to me but not to her.

Proverbs 21:25 talks about how it can be destructive to avoid work in our lives. Because God wants to work in and through us, there will be times when we need to work even when we don't feel like it. When we work, the Bible encourages us to do our work like we are working for God. (Colossians 3:23)

It's also a good idea to start thinking about work you may someday enjoy. I like work that involves interacting with people. My favorite jobs have been babysitter, selling clothes in a shop, greeting and seating people in a restaurant, youth and women's minister, school counselor, hospital counselor, and now I love working as a counselor at my own center and speaking across the country. See how all these jobs involve people?

Even when the work we need to do isn't always pleasant, it can be rewarding. Sometimes it can make us feel good just to get something we are dreading done and out of the way. When it's a chore that doesn't have to be done very often, we can also tell ourselves we won't have to face it again for a while. Psalm 128:2 talks about the joy that comes from our labor or work. I remember the first time I got paid for a job in college where I not only babysat but had to do some housecleaning, which isn't my favorite activity. I learned that hard work pays off and I discovered that I enjoyed cleaning for others more than I enjoy cleaning up after myself.

Embracing Joy

The next time you need to get some work done, try and make it fun. Ask a friend to join you. (I always found cleaning my room went faster that way.) Listen to your favorite music. Light a candle. Put on a smile, and as you do your chores or school-work, let God know that you are working hard for Him. He's a great boss.

Sharing Your Happy with God

Lord, sometimes I feel like working and sometimes I'd rather relax or play. No matter what my work looks like, help me to work as if I'm doing it all for you. Amen.

ALL OF ME IS HAPPY

LYNN

"Let all that I am praise the Lord; may I never forget the good things he does for me."

Psalm 103:2 (NLT)

I do this strange thing when I feel really happy inside. *Are you ready for it? Even my family doesn't know I do this!* I rub my hands together until my palms make a squeaky sound. Silly, I know! But sometimes, I just feel so happy, so excited, I have to do something because my happy heart feels like it will explode! It's like everything in me has to participate in my happiness.

Often, I recognize that the thing I'm happy about, such as my child coming home for a visit or getting to do something I've been waiting for, are gifts from God.

David has this level and awareness of happiness about the Lord. He says, "Let all that I am praise the LORD; may I never forget the good things he does for me" (Psalm 103:2).

Let all that I am . . . like my squeaky hands and my happy heart . . . praise the Lord!

Embracing Joy

Do you do something when you're really happy? Jump up and down? Clap your hands? Do it now because it will make you feel happy, and keep doing it. Just like circumstances can make us happy, when we pair a motion with a feeling, doing that motion can bring more happiness into our lives.

Sharing Your Happy with God

Jesus, thank You for the times when I am
happy. In Jesus's name, Amen.

16

HAPPY DEPOSITS

LYNN

"Every good and perfect gift is from above, coming down from the Father of the heavenly lights, who does not change like shifting shadows."

JAMES 1:17

Today, I'm making Happy Deposits in my journal.

What's a Happy Deposit?

A deposit means to place something for safekeeping or in trust. For example, say you are saving to buy something you want. You take the money you make doing little jobs or have received as gifts and put it in a bank account. This action is called a deposit. When you are ready to use it, the money is there for you.

When I make a Happy Deposit, I write in a journal about something happy that happened, a gift from God in my life. Then, on a future day, when I want to feel grateful or I am feeling sad and need a pick-me-up, I look back and read my Happy Deposits. Reading all of the good things that have happened in my past fills my heart with joy. It reminds me God has been faithful, giving me good gifts just like James 1:17 says, "Every good and perfect gift is from above, coming down from the Father of the heavenly lights, who does not change like shifting shadows."

The great thing about making Happy Deposits and writing down the good gifts God has given us is that reading them can make you happy over and over again. Today, I felt happy as I wrote down the good things that have happened in my life this year. Some day in the future, I will read about the things I did this year and feel happy all over again.

Now it's your turn!

Embracing Joy

There are so many ways you can make Happy Deposits. I have a little notebook, where I make mine. You could make them digitally in a document on a device. Any place where you can record the good things in your life is a great place to start making deposits. You can make your first deposit on the lines below right now. Here is an example of one of mine: *Thank you for such a wonderful Christmas! I think it was one of my favorites ever!*

....

....

....

....

Sharing Your Happy with God

Jesus, thank You for giving me happy days that I can record as Happy Deposits and save for reading later. In Jesus's name, Amen.

17 LET'S HAVE A PARTY

MICHELLE

> "And Nehemiah continued, "Go and celebrate with a feast of rich foods and sweet drinks, and share gifts of food with people who have nothing prepared. This is a sacred day before our Lord. Don't be dejected and sad, for the joy of the Lord is your strength!"
>
> NEHEMIAH 8:10 (NLT)

When something good happens in your life, how do you like to celebrate? If you could, would you get up and dance for joy? Is there someone with whom you would like to share your good news? Maybe you like to receive awards. Others love the idea of a party, inviting friends and family to celebrate with them.

Because I've been a counselor for over twenty years and spent lots of time in an office dealing with sadness and life troubles, I know the importance of balancing sadness with celebration. (Ecclesiastes 3:4) Rejoicing in God's blessings and goodness creates joy and places positive deposits in our life bank accounts. These deposits help us hang on when the troubles of the world create withdrawals.

For example, if I've had a bad day with lots of traffic making me late, and one of my kids gets upset because I forgot to stop and get them something they wanted, I remind myself of days when all the lights were green and how often I do remember to get them what they need. Other times when something is not going my way, I imagine how God could use these troubles for good in my future.

Embracing Joy

This week take time to look at photos with someone, remembering happy times and family celebrations. Then make plans to celebrate the good things that happen in your life and those around you. When life is busy, it's easy to ignore or barely acknowledge a holiday or important moment in life. The good news is it's never too late to celebrate! You don't even need a special occasion. I've had a party for my friends just to let them know how important they are to me. It also doesn't have to be a big party. My son and I have celebrated a positive moment in his life by getting ice cream and focusing on how hard he worked and how good life felt in that moment.

Sharing Your Happy with God

God, You are so good! We rejoice in You for being a God who desires to celebrate the blessings we've received on earth. We look forward to even more rejoicing someday in heaven. Amen.

18

GOD'S WILL FOR YOU

MICHELLE

"Rejoice always, pray without ceasing, give thanks in all circumstances; for this is the will of God in Christ Jesus for you."

1 Thessalonians 5:16-18 (ESV)

I used to think figuring out God's will for my life was the hardest thing in the world. Was I supposed to be able to read God's mind? I thought knowing God's will was like a target or bullseye I was supposed to hit, and if I messed up or missed it, I would not be doing God's will.

These verses in 1 Thessalonians give us a clear picture of God's will for all of us. I'm sure you will find practicing them as challenging as I do. We are to be glad all the time, always be praying, and give thanks no matter what comes our way. It's a tall order! But if we take it one at a time, it becomes much more manageable. I am learning to give thanks for every situation I face because they teach me more about God and myself. Over my lifetime, I've seen God restore even the biggest losses of my life. These verses teach us God's world view for living here on earth.

Embracing Joy

I love telescopes. They help me focus and that's a great thing because I'm easily distracted. How could you begin to take these verses regarding rejoicing, praying, and giving thanks and make them like a telescope when you look at your life? It might mean cutting out a lot of things you have been told are important by other people or movies and TV. You might draw a picture of a telescope or even look out of a real one this week to remind yourself to focus on things in God's will and ignore the distractions that crowd Him out.

Sharing Your Happy with God

God, I confess I often get distracted by things that don't matter. Help me become a person who makes time for You and spiritual moments in my life that help me know You better. I want to do Your will. Amen.

MORE AND MORE STUFF

LYNN

"You have given me greater joy than those who have abundant harvests of grain and new wine."

PSALM 4:7 (NLT)

Have you ever felt jealous? Do you ever feel uncomfortable when someone else is getting something new, appears to have more friends than you, or seems more successful?

Sometimes, when I see other people getting stuff I don't have and can't have, I struggle with jealousy. My brain thinks more means "happy."

When our hearts feel empty, we want more and more things to fill them up. We believe that more things will make us feel happier. It doesn't take long, though, for the shiny thing to shine no more and we're on to trying to get the *next* new thing. That's because every time we get something new it releases a feel-good chemical in our brain called dopamine. But dopamine only stays in our brain a short time and then our brain wants to make more so it wants another new thing.

In Psalm 4:7, David recognizes that it is God who gives something greater than things. He says, "You have given me greater joy than those who have abundant harvests of grain and new wine" (NLT). David's heart was filled with knowing just how much God loved him. This gave him more joy than having all the things.

The same is happening in my life. The more the love of God fills my heart, the less "stuff" I want. I am happy with what I have and that is a happy that lasts! Recognizing God's blessing over and over keeps the dopamine flowing in our brains.

Embracing Joy

Think about the last item you wanted. Do you still enjoy that thing as much today as the day you got it? Compare that thing to the love of God, which can fill our hearts every single day.

Sharing Your Happy with God

Jesus, thank You for loving me. Fill my heart right now with Your love. I want Your love to be what I want most, knowing it brings me lasting joy. In Jesus's name, Amen.

BELIEVING IN THE UNSEEN

MICHELLE

"Though you have not seen him, you love him. Though you do not now see him, you believe in him and rejoice with joy that is inexpressible and filled with glory."

1 Peter 1:8 (ESV)

My son and his dad both have scientific brains. They want to see things proven. I don't struggle with the idea of the unseen as much—maybe because I work with emotions and abstract ideas that you can't touch like love, fear, and connection.

Hebrews 11:1 defines faith as believing in the unseen. Even if you don't have a highly scientific brain, it's easy to doubt things you cannot see. There was a guy in the Bible named Thomas. When Jesus rose from the dead and appeared to His friends (often called disciples), Thomas doubted it was Him. Jesus understood and invited Thomas to touch His wounds.

Struggling with doubt can be distressing for many kids, but it's normal. I talk with students in middle and high school who have many questions about faith and what the Bible says. I encourage them to talk about this because wrestling with our doubts and seeking wise counsel from people of faith generally makes our faith stronger. When I meet kids who have shrinking faith, I often discover that they don't want to disappoint or upset their parents so they hide their questions. This can cause doubt to grow because it doesn't have a chance to be exposed to God's light. Jesus didn't freak out when Thomas doubted. He wants you to come to Him and let Him know when you're struggling.

Embracing Joy

As you have questions about your faith and things in the Bible that are mostly unseen, talk with a parent, Christian friend, or trusted adult at your church. Don't let your doubts steal your joy. Begin to train your heart to trust in an unseen God, learning to love Him and experiencing the joy that comes from choosing to believe.

Sharing Your Happy with God

God, sometimes I wish I could see You because life would be so much easier. Teach me to experience Your joy even though I can't physically see You. Amen.

WISDOM BRINGS JOY

MICHELLE

"Joyful is the person who finds wisdom, the one who gains understanding."

Proverbs 3:13 (NLT)

What is wisdom? Why would I want it?

I asked my son how he would define wisdom and he said, "Knowing meaningful things through experience." I liked his definition.

The next question is why would I want it? Proverbs 3:13 tells us that the person who finds wisdom, who gains understanding, is a joyful person. This is a great reason for wanting wisdom! Wisdom can come from learning from others who are older than you. You don't have to learn your own the lessons since they've already been taught. Wisdom is something I've continuously asked God for and He has been faithful to answer that prayer.

As a child, I enjoyed spending time around wise people who loved God. I babysat children of our church leaders who took an interest in my life. When I had questions, I talked with them and they shared about their lives when they were my age. I took the wisdom they shared and used it as I made life choices.

I hope you will find some older people in your life, whether a teacher or coach, boss or church leader who can mentor you. While my parents loved God and were leaders in our church, I am glad I got the opportunities to learn from the lives of others as well. I know that I'm more successful and our family is healthier because of the wisdom I gained along the way.

Who are the adults in your life that share their wisdom with you? My son used to stay after school and help one of his teachers wipe down the tables every day. During that time, they would visit together and she became an adult who shared her wisdom with him. My daughter has a vocal coach who encourages her to trust God when she is struggling with not being chosen to sing a certain song, play a certain part, or lead worship when she hoped to get the chance. She shares with my daughter about her own lost opportunities and how God used them to make her better. Sometimes she shares about how disappointments from when she was younger didn't really impact the life she lives now as an adult.

Embracing Joy

Make plans to talk with an adult—maybe even someone who's not in your family but who loves Jesus. Ask them to share some wisdom with you. One way I love doing this is to ask people, "What has God been teaching you lately?"

Sharing Your Happy with God

God, I pray that You would bless me with wisdom so that I will be more joyful. Please place people in my life whose experiences I can learn from so that I may be wise beyond my years. Amen.

22

YOU GIVE GOOD GIFTS

LYNN

"If you, then, though you are evil, know how to give good gifts to your children, how much more will your Father in heaven give good gifts to those who ask him!"

MATTHEW 7:11

Our family had planned a very special day of celebration that was going to be held outside. I couldn't wait for it to come! All week I had been looking at my weather app, trying to figure out what the day was going to be like. It kept showing rain plus very hot temperatures. I began praying, asking Father to stop the rain so our day would be wonderful. I thought no rain was best and kept trusting God to keep it away.

When the day arrived, the sun came out and I was so happy! But right before our event took place, the storm clouds gathered and then I heard it. Thunder. *Why are You allowing this to happen, Father?* I thought, as I looked out the window. I was devastated. But then, just a few minutes later, the rain stopped and I stepped outside. The air was cooler! The rain had actually dropped the temperature and brought a cooling breeze. This helped our special time together to be better than

I could have hoped for! We celebrated for hours, enjoying each other and the special day!

Sometimes our level of happy is determined by what we think will make us happy and so we ask God for those things.

I am discovering as I mature that God knows *exactly* what is best for us, even if it means something like rain before our special day. We can trust Him because our Father in heaven gives good gifts to those who ask him! And when He does bring the good we were hoping for, thank Him and be grateful for His wisdom and goodness!

Embracing Joy

Is there something in your life that you are asking God for or something you would like Him to do? Write out a short prayer below, telling God you trust Him with this, even if it doesn't look exactly like you are hoping or expecting.

....

....

....

....

Sharing Your Happy with God

Father, thank you for all the good gifts that bring happiness into my life. I can trust You with my happiness. You are kind and good and I trust You! In Jesus's name, Amen.

OBEY GOD AND BE HAPPY

MICHELLE

Some kids like rules. Rules feel safe to them. They know what to do and feel protected. Other kids find rules hard to remember and difficult to follow, which can lead to trouble. In the Bible, God gave the people laws or rules to follow because He knew His rules would help them live well on the earth He created. But like most of us, God's people struggled to follow or obey them.

Some of God's first rules I learned were the Ten Commandments in the Old Testament of the Bible. You can look them in up in Exodus 20:2–17 and Deuteronomy 5:6–21. In the New Testament, Jesus summed them up as love God and love others like you love yourself (Mark 12:30–31). Focusing our minds on loving God and others for periods of time can produce happy thoughts which lead to happy feelings in our hearts and the release of happy hormones in our bodies.

Embracing Joy

How could you work at loving God and others this week? A practical way I've learned to display love is through the five love languages. They are physical touch like hugs and snuggles, saying or writing words of affirmation or saying nice things about God or someone, doing acts of service, spending time focused on God or someone, and giving gifts. Think about how you could demonstrate love to God or someone else this week. Write down your plan so you will be more likely to follow through.

....

....

....

....

Sharing Your Happy with God

God, I want to love You and others more so I can experience the happiness and joy You created for me in my life. Amen.

REJOICE IN THE LORD

MICHELLE

"Rejoice in the Lord always. I will say it again: Rejoice!"

Pʜɪʟɪᴘᴘɪᴀɴs 4:4

Some kids swear to me they were born grumpy. I get it. Rejoicing may not come naturally to everyone. But we can train our minds so things that seem hard become easier. Math problems are a great example of this. It might seem impossible to learn all the math facts at first, but the more you practice them, the easier they get. Eventually you know them like you know your name.

I believe rejoicing in the Lord is something you can train your brain to do just like a math problem, but in order to do so you will have to make time for it just like you would any skill practice. Think of it like learning a play on the field or playing an instrument. It also may mean that if your life is already pretty full, you may have to give up some play, screen, or chill time to make the practice of rejoicing part of your everyday routine.

You might try pairing it with something you already do, maybe something that doesn't require a lot of mental energy, like brushing your teeth, folding your clothes, doing dishes, or walking to school. While doing these activities, focus your mind on the characteristics of God you are learning about in His Word. Rejoice that He is strong, powerful, and loving, as well as your help, shield, and light in the darkness.

Embracing Joy

What does it look like for you to rejoice in the Lord? How could you put this practice into your life on a regular basis? A great way to make sure you rejoice in the Lord is to make some goals to practice in your everyday life. Here are some ideas:

1. I will focus on one good thing about God as I get dressed in the morning.
2. I will focus on rejoicing in something good God has done for me when I take a bath or shower.
3. I will name a different characteristic of God I'm learning from the Bible every time I get in the car to go to church.

Sharing Your Happy with God

God, I live in a busy world that often distracts me from You. Help me set aside time each day to rejoice in You. Amen.

25

YOU'VE BEEN SO KIND TO ME

LYNN

> *"I will tell of the kindnesses of the LORD, the deeds for which he is to be praised, according to all the LORD has done for us—yes, the many good things he has done for Israel, according to his compassion and many kindnesses."*
>
> **ISAIAH 63:7**

Oh no! I thought as I continued pushing the button. Our clothes dryer wasn't starting. Even though I knew I was going to get the same results each time, I kept trying. Finally, I had to face it; our much-needed machine was broken.

Our family has a repairman we use that is very dependable, but lives quite far away. Picking up my phone, I texted him to get on his work list for his next trip to our town. "I'm in the neighborhood!" he texted back. I could hardly believe it!

Soon, he was in our home, diagnosing and fixing the problem. We were elated! "Thank you so much for coming today; what a blessing this has been!" my husband thanked him. "I guess that's what you call serendipity." Serendipity? Dictionary.com says the word serendipity means: 1) an aptitude for making desirable discoveries by accident or 2) good fortune; luck:

My husband and I both knew that the repairman being in our neighborhood when we needed him had nothing to do with luck! It was a gift from our kind Father and this gift brought us so much joy!

The rest of the day, we would look at each other, smile and say, "I can't believe the way the day turned out! Thank you so much, Father!"

When we recognize and give thanks to God when He is good and kind to us, it gives our joy a boost! It reminds us that we have a loving Father who is looking over us, taking care of us and sometimes chooses to bless us by solving our troubles quickly.

Embracing Joy

Reminding ourselves that good things are good gifts from our Father reinforces joy in our hearts. Read this verse out loud as a reminder to your heart today: "Every good and perfect gift is from above, coming down from the Father of the heavenly lights, who does not change like shifting shadows." (James 1:17)

Sharing Your Happy with God

Father, thank you for the good and perfect gifts you give
to me each and every day. Each one of them brings me joy.
Thank you for your kindness! In Jesus's name, Amen.

HOW TO BEGIN A RELATIONSHIP WITH JESUS

The very best place for us to start when it comes to managing our emotions is with a relationship with the One who created us. God made you so He could have a close relationship with you.

Here is a way to begin your relationship with Jesus. To help make it understandable, we've heard it called the ABCs of Salvation:

1. Admit

Admit to God that you have sinned or made bad choices. We are not perfect like God. God's Word says it this way: "For all have sinned and fall short of the glory of God" (Romans 3:23). The result of sin is that we are separated from God forever (Romans 6:23). We need a bridge between us because of our sin and God.

2. Believe

Believe that Jesus Christ is God's one and only Son and receive Jesus's gift of forgiveness from all your sins. Forgiveness means the sins or bad choices you've already made and the ones you will make are forgotten forever. This forgiveness is a gift that can't be earned by being good. It comes from God because He is good and wants us to be with Him forever. That's why He let His Son Jesus come to earth as a baby. We celebrate Jesus's birth at Christmastime.

Around Easter, we begin to talk about Jesus dying on the cross for our sins and rising from the dead. Jesus tells us: "For God so loved the world that he gave his one and only Son, that whoever believes in him shall not perish but have eternal life" (John 3:16). The word believe means to accept as true. If you accept the truth that Jesus was God's Son, died on the cross for your sin, and rose again, then the Bible promises you that you will go to heaven and be with God forever.

3. Communicate

Communicate about your faith in Jesus Christ as Savior and Lord to someone. After you have made the decision to accept Jesus Christ as your Savior, share your decision with another person. Tell your parent, pastor, or friend who also believes in Jesus so they can encourage you. "If you confess with your mouth, 'Jesus is Lord,' and believe in your heart that God raised him from the dead, you will be saved. For it is with your heart that you believe and are justified, and it is with your mouth that you confess and are saved" (Romans 10:9–10).

Beginning a relationship with Jesus is just that—the beginning. We hope this devotional and others we've written will help that relationship continue to grow as you learn to trust Him with your life and live as a follower of Jesus.

ABOUT THE AUTHORS

Michelle Nietert

Michelle Nietert has been a licensed professional counselor for over 25 years. She is the coauthor of *Loved and Cherished: 100 Devotions for Girls; Make Up Your Mind: Unlock Your Thoughts, Transform Your Life;* and *God, I Feel Sad*, part of the Bringing Big Emotions to a Bigger God series. A popular speaker on topics regarding mental health, faith, and parenting, she is a frequent guest on national television and podcasts, including her own "Raising Mentally Healthy Kids." She and her husband Drew have been married almost two decades and have two school-aged children.

Connect with Michelle at:
@Michelle Nietert on Instagram
https://YourMentalHealthCoach.com

Lynn Cowell

Lynn Cowell is part of the Proverbs 31 Ministries' ministry team. As the author of many books from devotionals for tweens to Bible studies for adult women, she writes for all ages. Lynn calls home North Carolina, where she and her husband, Greg and the occasional backyard deer are adjusting to life as "just us." Along with their three adult children and their spouses, the Cowells love hiking, cooking together, and anything combining chocolate and peanut butter.

Connect with Lynn at:
@LynnCowell on Instagram
https://lynncowell.com

Notes

Notes

Notes

Notes